HELLAS

HER MONUMENTS AND SCENERY

BY

THOMAS CHASE, M.A.

CAMBRIDGE
SEVER AND FRANCIS
1863

University Press:
Welch, Bigelow, and Company,
Cambridge.

Inscribed

TO THE MEMORY OF

CORNELIUS CONWAY FELTON, LL. D.,

TO WHOM,

AS GENIAL INSTRUCTOR AND EVER-FAITHFUL FRIEND,

THE AUTHOR IS IN GREAT PART INDEBTED

FOR HIS LOVE AND HIS KNOWLEDGE

OF THE ARTS AND LETTERS

OF GREECE.

PREFACE.

IT has been a labour that was its own reward to collect these notes of personal observation during a tour in Greece, and combine them with the results of some subsequent study of the principles of Grecian Art. The work was begun, and in part carried through the press, in the hollow calm of the last Presidency; but when the bitter truth was manifest that our republic was doomed to drink the calamities of civil war, the author threw down his pen, for he had no heart to dwell on other themes than the one object of all our interests and all our cares. Yet, having from the first cherished the conviction that it is a time no less of hope than of agony, and believing that his country's cause is the cause of culture and civilization, as well as of humanity and freedom, deeming it, moreover, the part even of patriotism for those who are devoted to letters or the arts to pursue their calling with no less vigour than before, after the lapse of a twelvemonth he resumed his task. And whither shall they who fondly hope that it may be granted them to make some slight contributions to that part of their nation's glory which is most real and most permanent, turn for instruction and for inspiration rather than to Hellas? She is a teacher of humanity for all ages, and her voice is not silenced by the clash of arms:

> "For Greece and her foundations are
> Built below the tide of war,
> Based on the crystalline sea
> Of thought and its eternity."

WEST HAVERFORD, PA., November 27, 1862.

CONTENTS.

HELLAS.

FROM NAPLES TO ATHENS.

"Yet to the remnants of thy splendour past
Shall pilgrims, pensive, but unwearied, throng;
Long shall the voyager, with the Ionian blast,
Hail the bright clime of battle and of song!
Long shall thine annals and immortal tongue
Fill with thy fame the youth of many a shore;
Boast of the aged! lesson of the young!
Which sages venerate and bards adore,
As Pallas and the Muse unveil their awful lore."

I HAD seen the exiled sculptures of the Parthenon in London, the Venus of Melos at the Louvre, — strayed among the solemn ruins and through the opulent galleries of Rome, — been admitted, as it were, to the very households of the ancients, in the disentombed cities of Campania, and beheld on their walls the reflected glories of Grecian painting, beautiful even in its decline, — gazed, too, at Pæstum, in that silent plain by the side of the sea, on a well-nigh perfect image of the Doric temple, simple and elegant, matchless in harmony and repose. Yet all these sights so rich in blessings to a young American scholar — the crown of youthful studies, the realization of boyish dreams — but inflamed my longing to wander in that land which in arts, in letters, in all that exalts and dignifies man as an intellectual being, was the mistress and teacher of Rome herself, and still sways her sceptre over the whole civilized world.

It was then with a thrill of glad expectation that, on the 4th of May, 1853, I found myself, without companion, on board of a French steamer at Naples, and on my way to the Peiræus. Soon we were floating swiftly over the calm, blue, bright waters of the Mediterranean, along the picturesque coast of old Campania and Lucania, while rocks and hills and water all were flooded with the soft and living light of an Italian afternoon. Our company presented that variety of nationality and character commonly met with on Mediterranean steamships. There was a tall, graceful, neat-limbed Arab from Algiers, with his red slippers, loose trousers, and closely fitting fez; a slight, black-eyed Mexican lieutenant of the navy; two Franciscan monks, missionaries from Rome to Constantinople, with shaven crowns, and wearing the coarse brown robe of their order, tied by a rope around the girdle, — mild, good-natured, unintelligent, dirty creatures; a Russian gentleman, who was returning to Moscow, after spending several years in the most important countries of Europe, and perfecting himself in their languages, all of which he spoke with the ease and correctness often observable in the educated of his nation; an Italian from Rheggio, who declared to me his enthusiasm for his country's friend, Lord "Bee-ron," and pronounced me happy that I was about to follow his footsteps in the "land of lost gods and godlike men;" an intelligent young Greek from Syra, — doing honor to Mr. Hildner's school, of which he was an alumnus, — who did battle, with some Frenchmen, against a thin, melancholy, black-faced Armenian priest, who told them it was a sin to read any book whatever, without first assuring themselves that it had the express sanction of the Church ; a few ladies ; and the usual number of swarthy Frenchmen, polyglot Germans, and respectable Englishmen with round faces and mutton-chop whiskers.

The next morning the mountain isle of Stromboli, the fabled home of Æolus, was close before us, a conical rock, rising boldly from the sea ; and Ætna showed his summit far in the south. A few hours more brought us to the Straits of Messina, with the far-famed rock of Scylla raising its head modestly enough beneath the highlands of the Italian coast, to the height of about two hundred feet, while to the right, between our ship and the long, low, narrow point of sand on the Sicilian shore of the narrow pass, was the site of the whirlpool of Charybdis. Even at the present day, small vessels are sometimes endangered by its eddies ; but it has long lost the terrors with which it is invested in ancient song, whether from the superiority of modern navigation, or from some of the geological changes frequent in this volcanic region ; and we noticed, as we sailed calmly over it, only a slight agitation in the water, contrasting with the unruffled surface of the broader sea. Hurl-Gate is at least as terrible as this fabled monster.

In the harbour of the pretty town of Messina, finely situated at the foot of an amphitheatre of high, precipitous hills, clothed with the rich green of luxuriant groves, and sprinkled with white villas, we lay several hours just outside of the sickle which curves to form the inner harbour, and then coasted along the Sicilian shore, with Ætna in view near at hand, on our left, — the calm and grand sovereign of its attendant mountains, its quiet summit exhibiting no signs of the recent eruption.

The very rough sea which the vessel encountered that night was a disagreeable change for us; but at an early hour the next morning we anchored in the harbour of Valetta, the chief town of the island of Malta. Taking a little boat to the land, and safely running the gantlet of the beggars on the *Nix mangiare* stairs, I found a pleasant, homelike feeling in wandering about this town, and hearing, in the shops and streets, the familiar accents of my mother tongue. The language of the natives, it is true, is a mixture of Arabic and Punic; and a barbarous Italian, also, is extensively spoken; but English is the language of the government, and generally understood by the tradesmen, of whatever descent. Clean streets and honest shopkeepers were another and most welcome novelty to one fresh from Italian towns. Valetta is built chiefly of a bright cream-colored limestone, a very beautiful building material; in the forms and proportions of its edifices, also, the town makes no little pretensions to architectural beauty. In the cathedral of St. John I admired the costly mosaic pavement, the vaulted aisles, and some of the paintings and statues; but the effect of the building is impaired by its heavily gilded ceilings, and excessive ornamentation. In one of the chapels, a massive bronze railing takes the place of one of solid gold which was taken by Napoleon when he plundered the church of its vast treasures in 1798. Against a railing of solid silver, in another chapel, which escaped pillage by being painted over, hang three large keys, — those of the gates of Jerusalem, Acre, and Rhodes. Costly monuments of the Grand Masters of the Knights of Malta are seen on every hand in this church, and in the crypt below, dedicated to their patron saint; while nearly the whole floor is covered with the sculptured effigies of members of the order, mostly concealed, except from the eyes of the curious traveller, by a matting of straw. In a hasty visit to the large public library, I noticed chiefly a small, but very interesting collection of fossil shells and fishes from the rocks of the neighbourhood.

We could stay but a few hours at Malta, for our steamer was behind her time, and the boat for Constantinople was waiting to receive us. Transferred to the large wooden steamer *Osiris*, before noon we were again ploughing the Mediterranean, with our prow turned to the East. What a glare of the sun, poured from a cloudless sky, and reflected from the sparkling waters; how we tossed on the cross, chopping waves of that midland ocean! On the morning of the third day we hailed "the bright clime of battle and of song;" for there, clearly defined in the early light, the hilly shores of Peloponnesus rose before us, and soon, passing the Gulf of Conon, we were off Cape Matapan, its barren, treeless hills standing out in bold relief beneath that brilliant sky, and the rock wall of their bases deeply indented by the gnawing surges. A long, low point of rock extends from these hills, and forms the southern extremity of the cape. We saw an old man walking on the shore, — a hermit, who had chosen for his retreat the southernmost point of Europe. It was not long before we were passing between the mainland and the barren hills of Cythera, — now Cerigo,— where, first of European Greece, the worship of Aphrodite was introduced by Asiatic colonists, or where, in the graceful language of mythology, she sprang from the foam of the sea. The deep-blue Ægean gave us a hospitable reception worthy of its ancient fame, in striking contrast to the stormy waters of the West. Over its hushed waves, amid its storied isles, we glided on to Syra, where we arrived at midnight. A boat soon came alongside from the shore, in which, by the light of a lantern they bore, we noticed an old man and a youth, clad in the peculiar and picturesque costume of these petticoat-trousered islanders. They endeavored to beguile passengers for the Peiræus to take their boat to the other steamer at that time; but as we knew it would not leave until after we had been admitted to *pratique* in the morning, they lost the opportunity of demanding an exorbitant price on account of the lateness of the hour. From this boat our ears were first saluted by the accents of the Modern Greek language; but, in our inexperience, we could distinguish little but the often-repeated word of assent, "Málista."

The town of Syra — the most important and flourishing commercial port of Greece — is built on the slope of a hill, surrounding a fine bay, on the eastern side of the island. It holds an enviable rank among the towns of the kingdom for the excellence of its schools, one of which, that under the care of Mr. Hildner, a German missionary, is among the very few allowed to exist in Greece without compliance with the law requiring the catechism of the Greek Church. to be taught in every place of instruction.

From this island we departed late in the forenoon, for the Peiræus, in the steamer *Lycourge*, the *Osiris* proceeding on her way, at the same time, for Smyrna and Constantinople. The detention which had abridged our stay at Malta gave us the unusual advantage of passing among the romantic " isles which crown the Ægean deep " by daylight, instead of in the night. Thus, in our passage from Cape Matapan to the Peiræus, we enjoyed a view of nearly every one of the Cyclades. The numerous small isles which form this group are rocky, hilly, and almost universally dry and barren in their appearance, but picturesque in form and outline, and grouped charmingly in the calm, blue waters of the sea, sparkling, in the flood of sunshine, like jewels on her breast. But their names, — the associations, — their immortal renown in history and song, — awakened all my enthusiasm as I floated by their shores. In grateful relief to the general barrenness of these islands, the long hill-sides of Zea (Ceos of old) are dotted with groves of Valonian oak, a noble tree, of dark green foliage. The picturesque outline of the southern shore of Eubœa soon greeted our eyes, and then the promontory of Sunium, the southeastern point of Attica, with the beautiful ruin of the temple of Athena gleaming from afar, diminished in the distance to a little speck of white. Those fair columns, hewn from the marble of a neighbouring hill, crown a cliff impending the sea in front of the higher eminence of the peninsula. An opera-glass assisted me in examining them. Even Turner's well-known drawing does scanty justice to their loveliness and the surpassing grandeur of their situation. As one passes by the side of the treeless hills, of lime-rock mingled with mica slate and clay slate, which form this promontory, called by the Grèeks of the present day Kávo Kolónai, — the Cape of the Columns, — the panorama is beautiful in the extreme. The picturesque outline of the hills of the Morea and the Isthmus in the distance, the lovely isles of Ægina and Salamis, the Acropolis, and the hills of Attica, under the soft light of the setting sun, whose last beams were painting the western skies with rose and purple and gold, upon a background of delicious apple-green, presented a picture of the most enchanting loveliness. A tall, slight, venerable Briton, who sat reading the London "Athenæum" on deck, had attracted my attention by his quiet, gentlemanly bearing, and his intelligent look. It proved to be Mr. George Finlay, the learned author of the "History of the Byzantine Empire," of "Greece under the Romans," and other well-known standard works, who was returning to Athens, where he has lived for many years, from a journey in pursuit of health among the Greek islands. Mr. Finlay, with a courtesy to a young stranger which evinced his kindness of heart, took pleasure in pointing out to me the many objects of immortal interest which we passed. As I was leaning over the side of the vessel after we had left Ægina behind us, he came to me and said, — quoting the lines of Childe Harold, — "Here *you* can say, —

'Wandering in youth, I traced the path of him,
The Roman friend of Rome's least mortal mind,
The friend of Tully: as my bark did skim
The bright blue waters with a fanning wind,
Came MEGARA before me, and behind
ÆGINA lay, PEIRÆUS on the right,
And CORINTH on the left:'"

the same "corpses of noble cities" which prompted those moralizing strains of Sulpicius, which we read on the old college benches. "Wandering in youth!" I repeated the words to myself, for I had been feeling lonely, and they suggested the high enjoyments of which a little loneliness and privation are only the necessary condition. As we enter the harbour, a sarcophagus, hollowed out of the rock at the water's edge, is seen, near which lie the fragments of a large column. This is called the monument of Themistocles,—most appropriately situated in sight of the scene of his great victory on the one hand, and the city he saved on the other. Mr. Finlay told me that he once made Lord Byron very angry by saying to him that he ought not to have spoken of the hero's tomb as standing

> "*High o'er the land* he saved in vain,"

but rather as *low in the sea.*

The entrance of the haven of the Peiræus is extremely narrow, but the harbour itself deep and commodious. Conspicuous among the vessels here sheltered was the American war-frigate Cumberland, whose fine model and beautiful proportions drew forth the most rapturous expressions of delight from some intelligent French gentlemen on board of our steamer. A French fleet, of some thirteen vessels of war, was lying in the Gulf of Salamis, awaiting, like the English fleet at Malta, the expected crisis at Constantinople. Taking a boat, I was soon on Attic soil; and, avoiding any detention with my luggage by leaving a drachma at the custom-house, was directly seated in a carriage, with Thessalian horses, and on my way to the venerable city of Athena. On we went, racing from the Peiræus to Athens; for my carriage had the start, and the drivers from other hotels were emulous; but, after several spirited trials, they abandoned the attempt to pass us.

"And this is Athens!" said I, not without surprise, when, after riding half an hour on the jolting and dusty road, we entered the narrow streets and began to pass the low, shabby shops and houses of the modern city. "And this is Athens!" I said, with a different feeling, a thousand times afterwards, when, in the early morn, or beneath the glories of a sunset sky, I gazed on the unrivalled loveliness of its ruined temples, or surveyed from its immortal hills the peculiar and enchanting landscape, — the heights, the vale, the picturesque islands, and the calm, blue sea. Even the modern city improves on acquaintance. In the quarter of the town near the Palace, wide streets are laid out, lined with large and commodious houses, and new buildings are erecting in great numbers. This activity in building, these signs of growth, and the bright colours and neatness of the houses in that neighbourhood, quite remind one of a thriving New England town.

But no one comes to Athens from more civilized lands to see the modern city. We come to examine the most beautiful and perfect remains of ancient architecture; to witness the scenes associated with the history, and immortalized by the genius, of heroes, bards, and sages; to realize the dreams of our youth, while standing with Demosthenes on the Bema, or Paul on the Areopagus, wandering with Plato in the groves of the Academy, or recalling the sublimest strains of ancient tragedy on the hill Colonos. And nowhere does the classic pilgrim find so many shrines to venerate,—nowhere can he so readily recall and recreate the past. The chief ruins in Athens are very fortunate in their position; in this respect, as well as in beauty, vastly superior to those of Rome. The city of the Cæsars can, indeed, claim pre-eminence in the extent and colossal grandeur of its imperial ruins; but, with some happy exceptions, they are so surrounded and obscured by tasteless, ugly, recent buildings,—there is such an incongruous mixture of the ancient and the modern,—that they do not make that uniform and homogeneous impression which one receives from the monuments of Athenian greatness. The beautiful and majestic columns of the Temple of the Olympian Jove stand, in solitary grandeur, on a broad, clean plain above the banks of the Ilyssus; the almost perfectly preserved Temple of Theseus displays its fair proportions, unhidden by inappropriate buildings; and the crowning beauty of the city, the abrupt, picturesque height of the

Acropolis, with its peerless temples, rising in bold relief in the transparent air of Attica, greets the eye, to delight and detain it, from every quarter, — whether one strolls in the groves of the Academy, or wanders by the banks of the twin streamlets of the Athenian vale, or stands directly under its shade on the summit of the Areopagus, or mounts the Bema at the Pnyx, or surveys the beautiful and storied landscape from the neighbouring eminences of Mount Musæum or Lycabettus, or the more distant heights of Hymettus, Pentelicon, or Ægaleus. There is no finer situation in the world than that of the Parthenon, as there is no finer edifice.

The officers of the Cumberland made a large and most welcome addition to the small society of American residents in this city during my visit. At a brilliant entertainment, which they gave on board the vessel, on Wednesday evening, the 18th of May, there were present not only the American ladies and gentlemen then in Athens or at the Peiræus, but one whose fame has been carried to the remotest corners of the civilized world, — Byron's "Maid of

Athens." She is now the wife of an English gentleman, and rejoices in the name of Blacke; her hair is still of the raven's hue, but years have robbed her of most of those charms which captivated the young poet. Those charms, however, cannot have exceeded, if they can have equalled, those of the lovely daughter of the "Maid of Athens," a young lady of about eighteen, who, as well as her father, mother, and brother, was present at this entertainment, and whose surpassing loveliness could subdue a far less susceptible heart than that of Byron. The object of the young poet's admiration was dressed in the French style, and wore a double band of gold ornaments around her hair.

I found a great interest felt by the Greeks universally in the difficulties existing in Constantinople, and great exultation in the rumours that Russia was ready to prosecute her demands, if uncomplied with, at the point of the sword. Fond dreams are still cherished of the re-establishment of a Byzantine-Greek Empire, — a "*νέον Βυζαντινοελληνικὸν Κράτος*," as the "Athena" newspaper hath it. Even if that be not accomplished, the Greeks hope to gain, from the fall of Turkey, at least a large extension of their territory. Some of their newspapers suggest that the best practical solution of all difficulties in regard to the balance of power arising from the fall of Turkey (a fall before many years inevitable, in the opinion of the best judges) will be the bestowal of its European territories upon the Greek kingdom. When the diplomatists of the Great Powers — or their statesmen, if such shall arise — find out that the interests of mankind and the true interest of their own governments are not opposed to each other, we may hope to see the end of that hideous anomaly in Europe, a small and imbecile Moslem aristocracy upheld by Western bayonets upon the necks of a Christian population, and to welcome that race to a large share of the political power of the Levant, which by its intelligence, its ability, its purer faith, and its preponderance in numbers, is so fully entitled to wield it.

ARGOLIS.

Τὸ γὰρ παλαιὸν Ἄργος οὑπόθεις τόδε,
τῆς οἰστροπλῆγος ἄλσος Ἰνάχου κόρης·
αὕτη δ', Ὀρέστα, τοῦ λυκοκτόνου θεοῦ
ἀγορὰ Λύκειος· οὑξ ἀριστερᾶς δ' ὅδε
Ἥρας ὁ κλεινὸς ναός· οἷ δ' ἱκάνομεν,
φάσκειν Μυκήνας τὰς πολυχρύσους ὁρᾶν.
SOPHOCLES.

GLAD enough was I, on the morning of the 21st of May, to leave the hot air and arid soil of Athens, for a short excursion in Argolis and on the Isthmus of Corinth. Rising before the break of day, our party, consisting of Mr. Blackie, the learned Professor of Greek at the University of Edinburgh, Mr. Clyde (a young Scotchman spending a year at Athens for the purpose of acquiring the modern Greek language),* and myself, with our intelligent

* Mr. Clyde has given the world some of the fruits of his diligent study, in an admirable pamphlet, entitled, "Romaic and Modern Greek compared with one another, and with Ancient Greek," (Edinburgh, 1855,) highly and justly eulogized by Lord Broughton for the "valuable information and sound criticism" it contains on the subject in question.

guide, François Vitalis, drove to the Peiræus, where we took the French steamer for Nauplia.

The deck of a steamboat on Greek waters presents a gay and novel scene to an American eye. Under the shade of the awnings, groups of men, women, and children may be seen lying on the Turkey mats, which they carry to enable them to spread a couch in almost any situation; some sleeping, some eating, or drinking wine from earthen bottles; others amusing themselves in conversation, or assisting their meditations by a pipe, or, more commonly, an extemporaneous cigar, made by rolling up a mass of the mild tobacco of the country within a piece of thin white paper. The bright hues and striking contrasts of colour in the picturesque costume of the men heighten its effect. A long woollen fez of bright crimson, woven without seam, falling gracefully over one side, and adorned with a tassel of blue silk, forms the head-dress; a full, spreading kilt or tunic of white linen, the fustanella, is the principal article of clothing for the body, relieved by a rich jacket or waistcoat, without sleeves, elaborately wrought of silk or worsted, blue, green, brown, black, or of several colours combined, and frequently adorned by ornaments in gold or silver thread. In front of this jacket a pouch or pocket is often attached, always highly ornamented. A red sash around the waist secures the graceful setting of the tunic, which hangs in multitudinous folds beneath. Fine white drawers are worn upon the legs, and rich crimson or scarlet buskins, of silk, or other delicate material, extend from the knees to the feet, which are clad in bright slippers. These buskins or leggings are elaborately wrought, and form one of the most striking parts of the costume. The dress I have described is the one worn by the more wealthy. Some wear garments similar in form, but of less costly materials; coarse leather buskins may be seen in place of elegant silk or woollen; a simple straw hat may be worn on the head; and various mixtures of the Frank and Greek costumes are noticed, while many Greeks adopt throughout the dress of Northern Europe. The lower orders to a great extent discard the more expensive and easily soiled tunic, and wear beneath their simple jacket an ungainly dress of dark cloth, extending from the waist to the knees, in form a ridiculous mixture of petticoat and breeches, — a garment that would put to shame Mrs. Bloomer herself. Below the knees their legs are bare. The waddling gait which they seem to have, as these broad folds flap about their legs, is anything but graceful. Their dark complexions, sometimes still darker than those of mulattoes, are another striking feature in the appearance of the groups on deck. The women are not remarkable for their beauty, and the old ladies are particularly hideous; the girls, however, are sometimes pretty, and the young men generally have agreeable, intelligent, and manly countenances, and are in some cases decidedly beautiful, — with bright eyes, rich complexions, and noble features.

The Greeks, wherever I met them, struck me as an intelligent race. There is, too, a manliness and self-respect in their bearing, which forms a pleasant contrast with the degraded aspect of the downtrodden inhabitants of the South of Italy. The latter people, in their appearance, realize most fully that eloquent description of the situation of the victims of oppression, "There is in their hearts no hope." * But the quick-eyed Greek walks erect in the proud consciousness of freedom, and points exultingly to the future, which is to develop the full resources of his country, and expel the yet lingering remains of barbarism. We could not but be pleased with the whole bearing of the bright-eyed fellows who clustered around us, and talked with great courtesy, and without reserve, of the condition and prospects of the kingdom,—boasting of their freedom from superstition and priestly domination, as compared with Roman Catholics, and urging their youth as a nation in excuse for the defects of their civilization.

Passing the islands of Salamis, Ægina, and Poros, we stopped a few moments at the beautiful town of Hydra, on the island of the same name, distinguished for its valour and sacrifices in the Greek Revolution. This town,

* God speed the day when this language shall be no longer applicable to the people of any part of Italy.

built of clean, white, comfortable houses, and rising in a natural amphitheatre on the sides of a barren but grand and picturesque hill, presents a beautiful and imposing picture. Another stop at the island of Spezzia, — which somewhat resembles Hydra, but is smaller and much less picturesque, — and we were within the lovely Gulf of Nauplia, the Sinus Argolicus. When we at length entered the harbour of Nauplia, a scene of unusual grandeur and beauty was spread before us. On every side, except where the plain of Argos meets the sea by the side of the town, rise noble mountains, which, though barren and unclad with trees or verdure, delight the spectator by that picturesqueness of outline and beauty of colour — blue and brown and gray and purple — which give the hills of Greece their peculiar charm. The bends of the shore afford the view of land on all sides, and it seemed as if we were floating on some grand mountain lake. Before us rose the precipitous and lofty rock of Palamídi, which forms the citadel of the place, — making Nauplia the Gibraltar of Greece. Another picturesque but inferior height, on its flank, is also fortified; and a little island, sleeping on the calm bosom of the water, is covered with a fort. A small but trim Greek corvette displayed the white and blue stripes and the blue cross, — the national flag, — which also waved from the fortresses. A few trading vessels and countless little boats lay in the spacious harbour. The town looked neat and pleasant from the water, and the rare but delightful sight of rich, green herbage was afforded by the long and grassy plain of Argos. And all was flooded with the light, and covered by the transparent vault, of a Grecian sky.

Refreshed by a good dinner at the Hotel of the Peace, *Ξενοδοχεῖον ἡ Εἰρήνη* (*sic*), we took an evening walk in the town and neighbouring meadows. Our hotel was on the principal square, which, surrounded with respectable buildings, adorned with plane-trees, and frequented by well-dressed citizens and soldiers, gave us a favourable impression of the place at the outset. Another but smaller square lies at the end of a street which runs from the centre of this one, and fronts the old palace of the king, a decent yellow building, two stories in height. We noticed, as we walked through the town, a certain style and elegance in the architecture, superior to the ordinary streets of Athens. The environs are well cultivated, and clad with grain, tobacco, grape-vines, currant-vines, and orchards of figs and mulberries. A large species of reed, very tall and stout, grows in the plain, and is often planted for hedges; and wild almonds abound. Water is found in abundance, and distributed by machines for irrigation: still in the land of Danaus survives the art he introduced. As we entered a garden to inspect a machine for raising water, turned by a donkey, the master and mistress of the house came out, and, with graceful hospitality, culled flowers and presented each of us a bouquet of exquisitely fragrant pinks and roses. In these groves we heard the shrill, clear song of the nightingale, and the sweeter notes of the blackbird; nor did we fail to notice the peculiar sound of the frogs, — most unlike their croaking in America, and which corresponds exactly with the description in the line of Aristophanes, and could not be represented better than by his phrase, "brekekekék, koák, koák."* The sound first named is the most sharp and shrill; the second the more deep. One of them is made by one gender of the amphibious musicians, the other by the other. I venture to pronounce the shrill "brekekekék" the voice of the female, for, as I stood one day by the ruined bridge over the Ilyssus, near the Stadium in Athens, I heard the two parties striving for the supremacy; loud and strong for some time both sounds arose in concert, — but at length the brekekekékers outstormed the rest, and their discomfited husbands gave them the field, uttering only from time to time, a discontented, but subdued and half-submissive "koak."

Returning to the square in front of our hotel, we joined a group of men, women, and boys, intently listening to the strains of a street

---

* Aristophanes writes *βρεκεκεκέξ, κοάξ, κοάξ,* using *ξ* to give the words a regular termination. The *ο* and *α* in *κοάξ* should be pronounced rapidly together, the *α* having the broad Italian sound. A strong stress should be placed on the last syllable of each word, as in the written Greek, — for the Attic frogs pronounce by the accents.

ballad-singer, — a modern descendant of the Homeridæ, — who, with lively gestures, was recounting how the great hero Marco Botzarēs slew forty Turks with his own hands at Mesolongi; and when he was surrounded by the enemy, told them that his name was Botzarēs, and he would not surrender.

Night brought with it its own peculiar classical reminiscences; for the "Bedouins from the bedpost," — as Felton translates *οἱ Κορίνθιοι*, in "The Clouds," — mustered in great force, and charged with more than wonted fury. We passed the dark hours in alternate battle and repose.

The next morning, having obtained permission to enter the citadel, we climbed the north cliff of Palamídi by a winding staircase, built on the sides of the precipitous rock. Eight hundred and sixty-four steps conducted us to the outer gate, and some two hundred more to the summit. A magnificent prospect rewards the toil of the ascent. The grand mountains of Arcadia, — the sides of one of which were white with snow, — of Laconia, and of Argolis lie around you on every side, with every variety of hue, from their different distances and different exposures to the rays of the sun, while the Bay of Nauplia stretches along at the side, its clear surface, as we saw it, agitated by not a single ripple, and in colour of the softest, lightest blue imaginable. Near the shore, where there was a transparent and singularly beautiful green hue in the slumbering water, boys were swimming, and their limbs flashed silver in the translucent element. The verdure of the great Argolic plain, in the foreground, on the side opposite the sea, gives grateful relief to the simple colours of the rocky mountains. The citadel itself was built by the Venetians, and contains a number of brass cannon, formerly belonging to their republic. It is at present garrisoned by a hundred and twenty-five or a hundred and fifty men. The prickly-pear grows abundantly on the rock; here, too, I plucked the delicate and exquisitely beautiful blossoms of the caper-vine.*

* I cannot forbear quoting Sig. Ruffini's description of this lovely flower: "He presently came out of one of his hiding-places, shouting and waving a huge bunch of flowers, so inconceivably gay, that they could only be met with, he declared,

After inspecting this modern citadel, we drove to one of the most ancient fortifications in the world, — the remains of the walls of Tiryns, *Τίρυνς τειχιόεσσα*, — "three thousand and two hundred years old" by mythical chronology. The walls consisted of two enclosures — an upper and a lower one — on the sides of a small, island-like hill, which rises steep and precipitously from the plain, and was occupied, as Curtius conjectures, as a fore-post of the Achaians against the Asiatic immigrants who stationed themselves in Nauplia. They are the best specimens extant of the fortifications of the heroic age, and are built in what is called the Cyclopean style, — of huge, irregular polygonal blocks of stone, without cement, the

---

on the way to the gayest village in the world. From the centre of each of the large white blossoms he held in his hand, there sprung up a long, elegant aigrette of deep lilac stamens. The ensemble, so rich and delicate, had a certain resemblance to the tail of a white peacock. "What can it be?" said Lucy. "It is the *Capparis spinosa*," answered Antonio, "and these flowers you admire so much are but capers in full blossom, best known for culinary purposes." — *Dr. Antonio*, p. 187. The white blossoms are faintly streaked with pink or purple. It is the unopened buds which are used for the table.

interstices having been neatly filled with little stones, most of which have fallen out. The size of the blocks is stupendous, — some being seven feet square, and others ten feet in length. They excited such wonder in Pausanias, that he says the smallest of them could not have been moved at all by a yoke of mules, and compares the whole structure to the Pyramids. The ground around is strewn with fallen rocks, and the walls still standing are in some places giving way. Two singular covered passage-ways or corridors, in the body of the wall, remain; the eastern one alone in any great completeness. It is curious on account of its arch-shaped roof, which, however, is by no means built on the principle of the arch, — the longest stones being used towards the top of the walls of the two sides, and their weight, where supported, compensating for the projection necessary to make the triangular form of the top of the chamber. The length of this gallery is about one hundred feet, its height ten or twelve, and its breadth five. There are six niches, or closed door-shaped windows, with arched tops, in the outer wall. For what purpose these galleries were built, is a puzzle which baffles antiquarians. Of the city, which was destroyed nearly five hundred years before Christ, no vestiges remain except the huge walls.

Among the ruins of the fortifications we noticed tall hollyhocks growing wild, and numberless thistles. The latter plant is found everywhere, and in great variety, in these regions. While searching for the entrance to the most ruined gallery, I was suddenly startled by being violently struck in the face by some tiny missile and a little stream of water. My assailant proved to be a harmless vine of the wild cucumber, which I had stepped upon, — a plant which runs upon the ground, and in its leaves and blossoms, and the shape of its fruit, resembles the edible cucumber. The fruit, however, is very small, and very prickly. When removed from the stalk, if sufficiently ripe, it ejects its seeds and a little water from the stem end with great violence.

An hour's drive farther, and we were on the site of the renowned old city of Argos, the cradle of Hellenic history. Of its ancient edifices there are hardly any vestiges remaining, except its vast theatre's sixty-seven rows of seats, hewn from the solid rock on the curving sides of a hill, and some parts of the wall of the citadel, crowning the lofty height of Larissa, behind the town. The modern village consists of a number of low huts, surrounded by pleasant gardens of mulberries and figs. Here we were reminded of Italy, by a troop of children who beset us, begging for five-lepton pieces (a small copper coin); but this was almost the sole instance of such an annoyance I met with in Greece; and, indeed, it was nothing compared with the insolent importunity of men, women, and children in an Italian town. We seated ourselves on the stone benches of the theatre, which in old time accommodated sixteen thousand spectators, and looked out on modern Argos. A glance at the ruins of a temple, in which the secret passage-ways of the artful priests have been exposed to profane eyes, and at the oracular cave of Apollo, and we were again seated in the carriage on our return to Nauplia. A young Greek whom we saw on our way,—the centre of a laughing group of youth, himself towering above them all, — in his manly frame, his black clustering hair, flashing eyes, and rich complexion, was the very incarnation of that ineffably beautiful Achilles of the Pompeian picture.*

The green marshes of Lerna, at the southern extremity of the plain of Argos, we looked at from a distance. They are the Hydra of mythology; its heads, their many fountains, of which if one were stopped others burst out elsewhere, till, by burning the woods which sheltered them, the mythic drainer and reclaimer of the land was enabled to conquer the monster.

The next morning beheld us, at about four o'clock, mounted on horses, ready for a long day's ride. Following the carriage-road until we came to Tiryns, we struck into a narrow path, which conducted us for a long distance over the plain to the neighbourhood of Mycenæ. Here we diverged, and, riding over several steep and rocky hills, soon found ourselves before the so-called Treasury of Atreus and

* The picture which represents Achilles delivering Briseis to the heralds who were to convey her to Agamemnon.

Tomb of Agamemnon. This is a great subterranean dome, fifty feet in height, and of about the same diameter, built of massive parallelogram blocks of conglomerate. A passage-way, twenty feet wide, protected on either side by massive walls, leads down to the building. Two slabs of enormous size form the roof of the entrance; the larger one is twenty-seven feet long, three and three quarters wide, and eighteen or twenty feet in horizontal thickness. Its weight, according to the calculations of the French expedition, is 372,000 lbs. What skill, and what powerful machines, must have been employed in placing it in its present position! The whole doorway is simple and massive; the effect of its proportions, half Egyptian, half Doric. Above the lintel is a large triangular opening. A vertical section of the dome would present a parabolic curve. The stones of which it is built are laid in regular circular courses, contracting as they rise, till the uppermost ring becomes so narrow that a single copestone (now displaced) capped the whole. In each course, the blocks touch each other with their interior edges, and for a little distance beyond, while the interstices left, as they extend outwards, are filled with small stones, driven in very compactly.

Even in its present naked simplicity, the effect of the grand structure is very imposing; but it was originally brilliant with ornament. At regular distances on the walls are seen the holes formerly filled with broad-headed brazen nails, portions of which still remain in a few places; fragments of plates of metal have been found in the building; and the conclusion is well established that the whole interior was originally lined with brazen plates, and formed a "brazen chamber," of the same character as those mentioned in the early legends of Greece. On the exterior, also, we find on the portal indications of former adorning. On each side of the doorway and above it are two wide parallel depressions, one within the other, in which the old ornamental facing was inserted. I noticed near either end of the outer one, above the doorway, a hollow in the rock in the shape of a pine-cone. These cones were so regular that they might almost be taken as designed themselves for simple ornaments; but they probably aided in the fastening of the external coating to the walls. There are nail-holes, too, on the exterior, particularly on each side of the triangular opening above the door. Moreover, fragments of semicircular attached columns, with zigzag ornaments, and of stone plates, were found in the excavations undertaken here by Lord Elgin. The stones were of various colours, red, green, and white; and the restoration of the old front of the building, which Donaldson attempted from these fragments, presents a quaint and rich style of architecture, unlike any that prevailed in Greece in the classic period, and reminding one rather of Oriental or Byzantine art.

We were admiring the simple majesty of the massive structure and the lofty dome, when the light from a fire of brushwood, kindled by François, attracted us into an inner cave, smaller than the other, and not constructed of hewn stone, but excavated in the crumbling conglomerate, which indeed is almost as soft and friable as earth. It is, by Curtius's measurements, twenty-seven feet long, twenty broad, and nineteen high. Over the entrance is a triangular opening, as in the exterior chamber. Antiquarians are divided as to the use of these apertures, — some thinking they were intended to receive sculptures, similar to that above the Gate of the Lions; others, perhaps with more reason, regarding them as designed to introduce light into the apartments. Our guide called this rude excavation Agamemnon's Tomb, giving the name of the Treasury of Atreus to the larger chamber; and he follows the judgment of some of the best scholars, in thus taking the inner room as a sepulchre, the outer as a treasure-house. From the earth above this ancient structure (which is so covered that one might stroll over the knoll with no suspicion of the wonder beneath, were his eyes not attracted by the walls of the passageway leading down to the entrance) I plucked some yellow flowers; and a beetle and other insects there congregated attracted our notice from their great size and bright colors.

Thence a short walk took us to the citadel, which was built on the summit of a steep hill, beneath higher mountains. The huge stone masses of the walls — in some places twenty feet high — produce a similar impression to that of the fortifications at Tiryns; and they present a very interesting combination of the three different styles of masonry found in the ancient Greek walls, — the Cyclopean (which is the oldest), in which huge irregular stones, unhewn, are piled together, the interstices being filled with smaller stones; the polygonal, of many-sided stones carefully hewn and nicely fitted to each other; and the rectangular, of regular parallelograms. But the great wonder of the place is the gate, formed of huge blocks, two upright and a third horizontal, over which are represented, in relief, two lionesses, standing, and resting their fore-paws on a pedestal whence rises a singular-shaped pillar, smaller at the bottom than at the top, and crowned by four round balls above its capital. This pillar, says Gerhard, is the symbol of Apollo Agyieus, or the protector of gates; and the lions, between which it stands, are armorial emblems of the Atreidæ: on the chest of Cypselus, Agamemnon has on his shield an image of Terror with the head of a lion. The heads are gone from the two lionesses; it is evident that they stood out boldly from the wall, in full relief, facing all who approached, emblems of formidable might. I have seen no monument of deeper interest than this, — the oldest sculpture in Europe, — the first bud of that flower which blossomed in the Parthenon. Rude as the lions are, they are highly expressive; "bones and veins and muscles are given with the closest adherence to nature;" and they breathe already that life and freedom which, subordinated to law, is the glory of Hellenic art. Moreover, in the solitude of their situation, in the thought that they have stood unchanged through so many generations of men, and in the imposing massiveness of the gate and walls they adorn, is a rare combination of impressive circumstances.

It was impossible to pass through this gate into the citadel, for the passage beyond was nearly filled with earth. The interior of the gate itself, however, had been excavated, and we stood under its massive portal, whence the King of Men sallied with his troops when he set out for the Trojan war.

In a little valley near at hand, where we found a well and a few willows, we reclined in the shade, and took our simple breakfast,—drinking water from a leathern bucket. Not a human habitation was to be seen on the site of mighty cities in olden time; a swineherd, tending his unpoetic charge, (although it, too, was suggestive of the Homeric times,) and a woman with a donkey, come to the well to get water, were all that broke the silence of the lonely spot. Spurring our horses, we set off at a full gallop over a beautiful plain, through which flowed a little stream, whose channel actually contained a good supply of water, unlike the dry beds of rivers we had passed.* The sight of the clear water and its pleasant murmur, the greenness of the shrubs and herbage, and, above all, the gorgeous splendour of a wilderness of oleanders,—whose bright and

* The mythic story of the punishment of the daughters of Danaus finds its explanation in the physical conformation of "thirsty Argos." "The numerous clefts and fissures," says Curtius, "greedily absorb the falling rain; but it flows rapidly away over the hard ground, and the thirsty land constantly pants anew for refreshment." Hence the necessity, and "the unthankfulness and toilsomeness," of artificial irrigation.

beautiful blossoms adorned the plain by the side of the brook, far and near, — exhilarated and delighted us beyond measure. Through wild, romantic glens we followed this stream for several hours, — crossing and recrossing it, plucking the magnificent oleanders, and filling our hats and bosoms with them as we passed, and gazing with awe and delight on the grand mountains which met the view in every direction. And such a sky! Heavens of the tenderest, most translucent *white*-blue, suffused with light, — an exquisite tint unrivalled elsewhere; and, floating in them, the most delicate little clouds.

At last we came to a little garden in the wilderness, with an humble khan for the accommodation of travellers; and here, in this beautiful oasis, beneath the shade of vines and fig-trees, we reclined and enjoyed a substantial lunch which our guide produced from his stores, and the no less grateful refreshment of a little slumber. But we were soon aroused, for we had a long journey yet before us; and, ascending and descending mountains, by steep, stony, unimaginable paths, sometimes following a stream flowing to the North, — for we had passed the water-shed, — we at length beheld, from the top of a hill, a grand, solitary valley imprisoned by mountains. In this vale rise three columns of an ancient temple, surrounded by the scattered remains of walls and pillars. They are of the Doric order, but of greater height in proportion to their diameter than is usual in that style. The pavement of the temple, and a few blocks of the lower courses of its walls, remain. They are built of a hard and coarse, but well-hammered stone. The effect of these graceful, solitary columns, in that grand and silent vale, as we galloped towards them over the long plain, or rode slowly among the fallen blocks which strew the ground around them, was most impressive. Retracing our course to the other end of the valley, passing some shepherds, whose rude huts were placed in the neighbourhood of their flocks of goats feeding in this solitary spot, and who offered us silver coins of Alexander the Great, we visited the remains of the great Theatre of Nemea, of which little more than the outline can now be traced, lying on the side of a hill. We were on the scene of the renowned Nemean Games; and no site could be more appropriate for such festivals than this magnificent valley. On the side of a high hill above the theatre, François showed us what is called the cave of the Nemean lion which was slain by Hercules. The old hero began to seem to us as a real existence, for it was not the first of the scenes of his exploits we had seen on our journey. We had been to Tiryns, where he was brought up; to Argos and Mycenæ, the home of his tyrant, Eurysthenes; from the hills of Argos we had gazed on the Lernæan Marsh, where he killed the hydra; and soon from the hills of Corinth we beheld Mount Cithæron, famed for his youthful prowess.

New mountains and ravines were to be passed before we reached Corinth. Our road was sometimes in the bed of a torrent, and always through wild and romantic scenery. The hills began to assume a peculiar appearance. Many of them are composed of masses of hard, white clay, rising precipitously from the ravines, and often most singularly covered at the top by a horizontal layer of sandstone. Through the clay soil deep gullies have been worn by the torrents and the rains. The sight of running water and the exquisite oleanders still gladdened our eyes, and at last we reached the final ridge which separates the Peloponnesus from the Isthmus, and beheld Parnassus in the distance, veiling in clouds his awful brow, Helicon, and Cithæron, and picturesque groups of other more neighbouring mountains, the bold height of Acrocorinthus, the modern town, and the long Corinthian Gulf. We entered the little town, and, in a clean and comfortable inn, enjoyed sound repose, after the fatigues of a twelve hours' ride. The next morning we visited the seven Doric columns, the very ancient ruins of the old Greek city, and, after a ride of nine miles across the Isthmus, with its picturesque dells and ridges, covered with grain-fields and dwarf pines, — glancing, as we passed, at the spot where the Isthmian Games were celebrated, and at the remains of the Isthmian wall, — took an Austrian steamer at Kalimáki for the Peiræus.

I could not tire of looking down into the water as we ploughed the Saronic Gulf. Its colour was an exquisite light blue, very like that in the Azure Grotto at Capri. The heavens were of a similar delicate hue; and a few light, lovely clouds hung in the blue upper sea.

After dining at the clean hotel, we took a boat for the tomb of Themistocles. Fragments, about twelve in number, of a large unfluted pillar of stone lie strewn around. Near it, two sarcophagus-like depressions are hollowed in the rock, and filled with the water of the sea. The column, from its size, must have been intended as a memorial of something; and it stands where rose the hero's monument, "by the sea's margin, on the watery strand."

FROM ATHENS TO PARNASSUS.

"Nullum est sine nomine saxum."
LUCAN.

WITH my agreeable and accomplished friend, Professor Blackie, I left Athens on the morning of the 2d of June, for a ten days' journey on horseback in Northern Greece. Besides our dragoman or guide, we were attended by the "master of the horses," a chief cook, an assistant cook, and two servants in charge of the three mules which carried our beds, provisions, and clothing. Rising at early dawn, after refreshing ourselves with a cup of black coffee and a slice of bread, it was our custom to set out with the first rays of the sun, and ride for four or five hours, till we reached some khan, where, beneath the shade of a tree, the table our dragoman carried was spread, and the best of breakfasts furnished by our skilful cooks. Our eager appetites appeased, rambles at will among the rocks, *mollesque sub arbore somni*, beguiled the hours till the heat of mid-day began to abate, and we mounted again for another ride of four or five hours, to our stopping-place for the night. This was generally a kind of khan, where the cooks found a kitchen of which they could have the use, and an upper chamber was ready for our beds. Our guide carried cot-bedsteads and good beds, with flannel blankets and other clothing, so that in these rude apartments we passed the nights in entire comfort. A family owning the house is generally found in the room which serves for the kitchen. In our bedroom, or in the open air, as we chose, the dinner-table was spread, with luxury as well as abundance; indeed, as, seated on our camp-stools, we partook of the six courses, we sometimes thought we would gladly exchange them for fare more congenial with the wildness of the scene. We gave the cook, however, in the most intelligible way, the compliment of thorough appreciation, remembering the dictum of physicians, that a generous diet is the best for travellers in hot countries. Dining with the first even-

4

ing shades, a ramble in the neighborhood to explore whatever is of interest to be seen, or a talk with the people, particularly with the Greek boys, who are very intelligent and better educated than their elders, and then the welcome couch. Such is the outline of a day's life. But how shall I describe the wild grandeur of the hills and mountains of Greece, the calm beauty of her plains, the transparency and delicious blueness of her sky, the delight, the exultation of bounding o'er her "haunted, holy ground," where every scene is hallowed by the most fascinating associations, and there is "no rock without a name"?

It was a fine morning when our cavalcade left the city of Theseus, and took its way through the olive-groves which border the streamlets of the Cephissus, vineyards, and fields of maize, and by the farm and neat country-house of the Queen, to the impregnable height of Phyle. By and by large pine-trees, scattered here and there by the road, afforded a pleasing contrast in colour with the olives. A picturesque pass, through hills dotted with shrub pines, leads into the range of

Parnes, which stretches, in complicated windings, from Cithæron to the east, a natural bulwark of Attica. Here, in a valley among the wild hills, we breakfasted in the pleasant village of Kassia, at an humble cafinet with no floor but the earth, in front of which we were accosted by the demarch of the town. Thence through grand ravines, — savage hills all around, the gray and brown of their rocky sides relieved by little pines, — having at our right the abrupt, double plunge of the mountain, forming the precipitous wall of a gorge, and passing through a valley gay with oleanders, we rode to the bold rock, with its table-like top, which the fortifications of Phyle crown. The high and precipitous eminence is inaccessible on two sides, and protected by walls on the others. Portions of the walls are in good preservation; they are built of large, regular blocks of stone, in two courses, the space between (which is very broad) being filled with a compact mass of large stones irregular in shape. A more secure retreat than this mountain fastness could not be imagined. To the lover of scenery, its historical associations are Phyle's least attractions; from its reverend brow we looked out upon a broad and beautiful landscape, embracing queenly Athens, Hymettus, a part of Eubœa, and the island-dotted sea. Over the old walls of the fort grow ivy and thorn-bushes. The wild glen which almost entirely surrounds the rocky citadel is one of singular beauty and grandeur; but it is even surpassed by the glens a little beyond Phyle in the same pass. Continuing on our way over most picturesque hills, clothed with pines, a plant resembling box, and thick-leaved holly-like shrubs, we soon had a fine view of the strait and island of Eubœa, and of a wide Bœotian plain, into which we descended. Passing a village at the right and two hamlets at the left, we dashed on to a little town, at the extremity of the plain, called Dervenosálesi, near which stands a ruined castle-like building of the Middle Ages on a romantic rocky height. The room we occupied for the night contained a rude painting of St. George, with a lamp hanging near it; the mistress of the house kneeled and crossed herself before the image of the saint, before retiring to rest.

The next morning, a little after four o'clock, we commenced the ascent of the stony, difficult hills which bound the plain, and soon from the summit of one of them saw distinctly Cithæron, Helicon, and the far-distant Parnassus. An intervening plain through which flows the Asopus, — a considerable stream, — and another ridge of hills, and we then looked down on the broad and fertile fields of Thebes. Descending, we crossed the Ismenus, a full stream, turning many mills; and another stream flowing from a large basin, with whose pure, cold waters we refreshed ourselves and our horses. We came soon to the moderate hill which was the Acropolis of the old city, and is the site of the modern town. It is of elliptical form, sloping to the north, and rises about one hundred and fifty feet above the plain. Renowned as was seven-gated Thebes, hardly a vestige of its ancient edifices survives. Pitiful pieces of marble from old buildings, it is true, are embedded in the rude walls of the modern houses; and large regular blocks of stone, with a few fragments of pillars and architectural ornaments, may be seen in the ruins of an old Turkish tower, a pier of a bridge, and a dilapidated church. We breakfasted at a khan, in the middle of the town. Modern Thebes presents the appearance of considerable activity and prosperity. The one-story shops and houses on its principal street are generally furnished with awnings of board, — no small convenience in this climate. There are good schools here, and we met some intelligent representatives of the Theban youth, one of whom had read at his school two books of the Iliad.

The arid summit of the Cadmeia was almost destitute of herbage. I succeeded, however, in finding a little flower, which, with others gathered at interesting points in my tour, has been given by the wife of our then Minister to Constantinople to a poetess almost as distinguished for her scholarship as for her extraordinary genius, — Mrs. Browning, — the modern Sappho,

"with aureole
Of ebon locks on calméd brows."

The plain around Thebes is not only fertile, but well cultivated. After descending and crossing a little streamlet,* we soon came into a region of secondary hills, — not of barren rock, like their loftier neighbors, but covered with light friable soil, and clad with waving grain, grass, or low shrubs, — actually green all over. Refreshed by their novelty and verdure, we wound our way around and over them, till we came to the plain of Thespiæ, at the extremity of which, on two little hills, is the village of Eremókastri, our halting-place for the night. In the plain are foundations of ancient structures, one of which our guide called a bath, and the other a temple, and in the walls of a neat, whitewashed church, which

* This brook, which flows to the northward, and empties into the Ismenus, is generally called Dirce by the topographers. As we were approaching Thebes from the east, I was repeating that magnificent ode from the Antigone, Ἀκτὶς ἀελίου, and was struck by the fact that the poet speaks of the rays of the morning sun as coming over the Dirce's waters, Διρκαίων ὑπὲρ ῥεέθρων μολοῦσα. Was the poet regardless of the actual situation, or can we give the name of Dirce to the streamlet and fountain directly east of the town?

I may allude here to the great pleasure it was, in many places on my journey, to recall lines which old school and college studies had fixed in my memory, in the very scenes which they describe.

stands by itself on a hill near the village, some spirited bas-reliefs, as well as vine-leaf ornaments, and the inscription of an old sepulchral monument, have been inserted. The most charming thing at Eremókastri is the view of Helicon and its neighbouring hills. The poetic mountain, as seen from this village, presents the appearance of a large cone, not unlike Vesuvius in shape, with a long ridge running easterly, terminated by another and smaller cone-like elevation. Its gray sides are dotted in many parts with trees, and trees appear to grow upon the very summit. But the hills running out to the north or northwest of the highest peak of Helicon present the most diversified, bold, and picturesque outline imaginable. As we watched them, reclining on our carpets, after dinner, upon a little hill in front of our khan, their lines, now waving, now jagged, drawn in bold relief against the evening sky, and their summits radiant with tenderest hues in the sunset glow, they made the fairest picture of the kind on which my eyes ever lingered. Long did we gaze on the scene, till the gathering shades obscured its beauty, and aloft, near the summit of Helicon, a red light gleamed forth from a monastery embosomed in that inviolable seclusion.

The beauty of the flowers and insects we met with on our excursion was a constant delight. In this day's journey, I plucked the most exquisite blue larkspurs, white and lilac candy-tuft, nutmeg honeysuckles, bachelor's-buttons, and mourning-brides.

Pursuing our way the next morning, we soon reached a height whence we had a view of the so-called Copaic Lake. How in the world, in a land so destitute of water, a lake of the grand dimensions which Copais exhibits on the maps could be found, had been a mystery to us; but what was our surprise, when, instead of a noble expanse of the liquid element, we looked down upon a broad, green plain, covered with grass and standing corn, grazed by large herds of horses and cattle, and only intersected here and there by a few small and sluggish rivers; — no Scotch mountain loch, or bright New England lakelet, to inspire delightful recollections of our native lands, but an immense swamp, nearly dry, very like some portions of the Pontine Marshes. In the winter, however, the lake better deserves its name. Breakfasting at a pleasant khan at its margin, we galloped entirely across the cracked soil of the wide, green limne, fording four or five muddy rivers. We disturbed the solitary rambles of a stately heron, and started up three or four noble eagles, who rose in silence, and winged to the north. Crossing the Cephissus by a bridge, we came to a village occupying the site of old and wealthy Orchomenus, on the side of Copais, and beneath a high hill still crowned by the remains of its citadel. Here is the so-called "Treasury of Minyas," almost the sole relic of the prehistoric grandeur of a rich and powerful city. It is a subterranean chamber, resembling the Treasury of Atreus at Mycenæ ; but the stonework of the top of its vault has been removed, and earth filled in, so that nothing is now visible save the upper part of its massive gateway, spanned by an immense block of limestone, whose under surface is coated with smooth cement. This block is about three feet above the present surface of the ground. It is sixteen feet in length, eight in breadth, and above three feet in thickness; there was probably another slab in the architrave. The site is on rising ground, a little above the valley, here filled with olive-trees.

Orchomenus was a principal seat of the worship of the Charites, or Graces, whom Pindar invokes in his fourteenth Olympic: —

> " O ye, that by Cephissis' waves profuse
> Dwell on the banks with steeds and pastures fair,
> Illustrious queens of proud Orchomenus,
> Listen, ye Graces, to my prayer.
> Ye whose protecting eyes
> The Minyans' ancient tribes defend,
> From you life's sweets and purest ecstasies
> On man's delighted race descend.
> Genius, and Beauty, and Immortal Fame
> Are yours; without the soft, majestic Graces,
> Not e'en the gods, in their celestial places,
> Or feast or dance proclaim."

The Copaic Lake (or Cephissis, as it was more anciently called) produces (particularly in the neighborhood of Orchomenus) a reed which has been properly reckoned among the most important productions of Bœotia, as affording the material of which the flute was made, by whose use her minstrels were distinguished.

> "Through vocal vent its music flows,
> Of brass with slender reed combined,
> That near the festive city grows,
> Where with light step the Graces move,
> Marking the measured dance they wind
> In cool Cephissis' flowery grove."

There were annual festivals in honour of the Graces at Orchomenus, and these flutes were used in the musical contests. The sanctuary is supposed to have been on a site now occupied by a monastery. Here we found an interesting collection of remains of the old city, — a grand old altar, adorned with three deers' heads, with garlands depending from their antlers, and bearing a long inscription; another altar, very large, which has been severed in the middle, and now forms two altars in the church; a statue in an Egypto-Greek style; a headless warrior; a torso; and a bas-relief in the interior of the church, supposed to be of the three Graces. Among the grotesque paintings of saints with which the sides of the church are lined, I was attracted to one of a young man with a pleasing face, represented in a modern Greek costume, and wearing arms. This is St. George the Young, a priest who fought in the Greek Revolution, and was canonized for his heroic exploits.

Again plunging into the plain, a ride of about two hours brought us to Lebadea, — green, delightful village, with groves, and gardens, and full, babbling streams of water, — an oasis in a thirsty land. Fording the copious stream of its river, we followed up the bed of a little brook, through groves of figs, vineyards, and banks gay with flowers, till we reached the hill on whose sides the town is built. The streets are paved with large, irregular stones, slippery and disagreeable to the horses. The town is large, and one of considerable trade and activity. Awnings are spread across the street in many places; the houses are open, and furnished with balconies, with quite an Oriental aspect. Our eyes gladdened by its rich verdure, and our ears by the rushing sound of its full, rapid streams, we were charmed with Lebadea, and gladly accepted it as our halting-place for the day of rest. In a wild gorge, near the town, beneath a precipitous mountain, crowned by well-preserved mediæval fortifications, the river bursts forth suddenly and violently from the foot of the rocky height, — a striking phenomenon, of which there are many instances in Greece.

The rocks in this wild, romantic gorge contain several caves, and many niches artificially excavated to receive statues and votive offerings; for here was the sanctuary and oracular cave of Trophonius. The precise position of the cave has not been ascertained, nor is it known which are the waters of memory, and which of oblivion; but the *religio loci* is still extremely impressive, and one cannot but acknowledge the fitness of the scene to impress with supernatural influences the lively susceptibilities of the Greeks. As we sat on the rocks by the gushing river, two bright-eyed, intelligent boys joined our company, with that easy but courteous freedom characteristic of this people, and sang Greek serenades and stirring patriotic lays, which my companion acknowledged by a spirited German song. These lads, one of whom was very handsomely clad in the full Greek costume, were noble-looking fellows, and particularly manly and graceful in their manners. We noticed in the Greek men, in general, a proud and independent, but very easy and graceful carriage, and a bearing which happily unites manliness and courtesy.

Beyond Lebadea, the hills were variegated with the bright yellow blossoms of a kind of broom, with thorn-like leaves. Singular fossils, resembling in shape the horns of some animal, (orthoceratites, probably,) abound in the road. We soon reached the plain of Chæronea, the scene of three important battles. Here, in the centre of an excavation in a little mound, not more than half a mile from the modern town, lie the fragments of one of the most impressive sepulchral monuments in the world, — the colossal marble lion erected over the remains of the Bœotians conquered by Philip in "that disastrous victory fatal to liberty." The stone is of a light slate-colour, and overgrown with gray lichens. Though the statue has been blown to pieces, — in the hope, it is said, of finding concealed treasure,

— the head is still perfect, and some of the legs and other portions; and this intensely interesting work of art might easily be restored. The gnashed teeth, the fiery eyes, the grand expression of a lofty spirit, unconquered in defeat, render this lion's head one of the most striking and noble sculptures of antiquity; nor could we behold without deep emotion, as we stood by the grave of those brave men, this wonderfully appropriate monument to their spirit and valour, as admirable in defeat as in success. At the town, which we reached in two hours from Lebadea, we found well-preserved remains of the walls of the double-peaked Acropolis, and a small theatre, excavated in the solid rock, on the sides of the hill, — the seats well preserved, although their marble coverings are gone, and the two præcinctions, or divisions between the seats of the different orders of spectators, high and well-marked. Some lads followed me to the top of the Acropolis, and sold me a few coins and a cameo head of Minerva. They gave their names as Achilles the son of Johannes, and Sōtēr the son of Athanasius; and in return I gave my own name and patronymic, in the same primitive style. In the plain, just below the village, is an old fountain, near which is a sarcophagus, with a cavity some four feet long and two and a half wide, bearing an inscription to some one called a Platonic philosopher; and there are many fragments of pillars of granite, resembling the beautiful stone quarried at Quincy. We had a brilliant, yet soft and mellow sunset, of red and yellow ethereal flame.

Our horses ran away in the night, and while we were waiting for their recapture we talked with some rustics seated on benches in front of the tax-gatherer's shop, — one of whom had a cane which excited our cupidity, though the old man could not be tempted to sell it. The handle was the representation, carved in wood, of the head of a bald Egyptian priest; on one side of the cane was carved a full-length figure of a man, with the inscription "Adam;" on the other, a woman, labelled "Eve." Beneath, there were two other figures, representing children of our great ancestors. Below was carved, in bold characters, the inscription borne on policemen's staves in Greece: "The power of the law," with this addition, "for boys and dogs;" — *ΙΣΧΥΣ ΤΟΥ ΝΟΜΟΥ ΤΩΝ ΠΑΙΔΩΝ ΚΑΙ ΤΩΝ ΣΚΥΛΩΝ.*

From Chæronea we pursued our path through romantic hills and plains to Daulia, the ancient Daulis, at the foot of Parnassus, — passing on our way the conspicuous walls which crown the lofty acropolis of Panopeus. Delightful Daulis! Thy bright, joyous brooks; thy green meadows; thy gardens of fig and peach, and groves of pomegranate, — the beautiful pomegranate, with its bright-green, glossy little leaves, and blossoms of gorgeous scarlet with yellow stamens, — form a picture of loveliness and fairy-like enchantment that will never fade from my memory. At this flowery hill-side we commenced the ascent of the haunted mount of song; and all was "one vast realm of wonder," as, through mountain gorges and over grand ridges, we wound our way along to the vine-clad heights of Aráchova, and thence to the cloud-capt summit of the sacred hill.

ASCENT OF PARNASSUS.

At Aráchova we exchanged our horses for mules, —

("On Parnassus mount,
You take a mule to climb, and not a muse,
Except in fable and figure,") —

and struck into a steep path, winding through vineyards, along the precipitous sides of the mountain, by which we soon gained a height commanding a large valley on the other side, fertile and well cultivated, though at so great an elevation, and diversified by a little summer-village of stone, windowless houses, and two small sheets of water. We had now left grape-vines and cultivation beneath, and, turning to the right, soon entered a forest of noble trees of spruce-fir, with long beards of gray moss. Before us, on a little donkey, followed by her colt, a pretty, bare-headed boy of about ten years sat sideways, breaking the stillness of that solitude by piping sweetly on a shepherd's reed; we longed for a painter to perpetuate the scene. Up and down, up and down rocky hills, and through evergreen groves, we pursued our way, till from one of the heights we looked into a large valley, surrounded by rocky, but tree-clad hills, whose summits formed the limit of trees on the mountain. Near the centre of the vale was a rude hut, built of stones picked up near by, and covered in part by boughs of fir, in part by an awning of black goat's-hair cloth. In front was a merry group of shepherds, amusing themselves by spinning around on a long, horizontal pole, attached by a pivot in the centre to a perpendicular post firmly planted in the ground, and allowing to those lying over either end, or hanging from it, a combined rotary and see-saw motion. Our little minstrel let his donkeys loose to feed, and joined this pastoral party, who soon dispersed to collect and milk their large flocks of sheep, feeding on the surrounding hills. The simple repast provided by our attendants was enriched by delicious draughts of fresh milk, presented by the shepherds, and new cheese-curd. Fresh boughs of spruce-fir were brought from the neighbouring hill-sides, and spread on the ground, under a large tree near the hut, for our beds. A large fire of dry boughs was kindled at our feet; and, covered by thick capotes, we slept soundly beneath the clear, star-studded sky, in the pure air and dewless night, lulled to rest by the musical tinkling of the sheep-bells, the sweet sounds of the shepherds' reeds, the clear cry of the cuckoo, and the watch-dogs' honest bark re-echoed from the mountains. Reclining around the fire, the shepherds told their robber tales far into the night; then sleep came over them, and no human sound broke the sublime stillness of the mountain solitude. Never have I enjoyed sweeter slumbers. Gently and imperceptibly I fell asleep, with none of the stupidity and heaviness which often brood over civilized chambers; and awoke to greet the divine dawn with clearest head and most elastic pulses.

At the first morning light, we again mounted and set out for the summit. Soon reaching the limit of trees, we beheld the long, gray ridges of Parnassus stretching far above us, with little patches of snow nestling in the hollows on their sides. Still up and down, by the rocky path, till the great backbone was reached, and, leaving the donkeys, we planted our feet on the everlasting rock, and pursued our way to the exulting peaks. By the side of minute streams, trickling from deep snow-banks, we picked delicate crocuses, violets, and other flowers of lovely hue, some of which had climbed to shed their beauty upon almost the highest summits. At last, a glorious panorama, interrupted only in small parts of the horizon at the southeast, where a peak a little higher than that on which we stood, but inaccessible on account of the snow and ice, obscured the view. All Greece lay outspread around us. Far in the north, blue in the distance, but distinct and well defined in the clear atmosphere, rose grand and beautiful Olympus, its many rolling peaks gleaming with snow. A little to its right, the prominent cone of Ossa stood conspicuous, and, next, the range of Pelion; on the left, the long chain of Pindus, the huge backbone of Greece, with

Othrys running from it to the east. The Gulf of Zeitun, beyond Thermopylæ, Eubœa, with the bright sea on either side, (for we could look entirely over the island,) and some of the isles of the lovely Ægean, adorned this side of the picture. At the west rose the mountains of Acarnania and Ætolia, their summits snow-clad, and their sides exhibiting a rich variety of colours, in the rich deep red and brown and gray of the lower region, the green trees of the central belt, and the broken rock and snow of the upper heights. To the south the Corinthian Gulf stretched out in long extent, its waters of that soft blue, bathed in the intense light of a Greek sky, characteristic of Greek seas. Beyond were the mountains of the Morea, bold and varied, with snow glittering on many of their summits, and their sides of various hues. And all these colours in the richly variegated landscape were embraced and canopied by the profound blue of the sky, in which, near the horizon, a few long clouds were suspended, of delicate texture, and with most exquisite blushes welcoming the early beams of the sun.

When at last we had bidden farewell to the snow-banks ten and fifteen feet deep, and farewell to the peaks which had sprung to the height of nearly eight thousand feet above the neighbouring sea, new beauties in the landscape unfolded themselves as we descended the rocky sides of the mountain. As we reached the region of trees, a thousand exquisite little pictures of wild glens of green and gray, fantastic branches, and intermingling outlines of rock and tree, met our eyes; of the blue gulf, nestled amidst embracing mountains, and sleeping like an inland lake; of town and cultured slopes, of rugged cliffs and snow-clad peaks. Then what a home-like feeling as we greeted the dear valley of our last night's rest, the quiet shepherds, and the tuneful flocks! Here we again sat down on the evergreen boughs; and, while we appeased our hunger, listened to the song of birds above our heads, the mellow notes of the shepherd's pipe, and the soft tinkling of the sheep-bells, and watched the shepherds beckoning their dogs to guard the flocks, or chatting on the grass before their rude hut. For the first time I gave full credence to all that poets have sung of the felicity and peace of pastoral life.

Descending to the plain, with its little village, which we noticed in the ascent, we rode across it, and climbed a very steep hill, near whose summit is the Corycian cave, sacred to Pan and Corycian nymphs; but more interesting in its poetic associations than in itself. It is a tolerably large grotto, with a slippery bottom, and a noble roof adorned with stalactites of graceful form but dull colour. Again, over hill and dale, among large trees of a holly-leaved oak, we came at length to the precipitous descent, which zigzags down the steep side of the mountain to Delphi. Down this we walked, the slippery path and rude stairway being too suggestive of broken necks for riding.

Kastri, as the modern town is called, is a dirty, straggling village, with narrow break-neck streets, and in every respect — except its delightful situation — as unpoetic in its aspect as possible. Women washing dirty linen at a public fountain in one of the streets — the Cassotis — suggested, both by resemblance and by contrast, the princesses of Homer. The ancient city of Delphi rose in a fine natural amphitheatre, on the side of a mountainous height, which is connected with the range of Parnassus, and, with the opposite wall of Mount Cirphis, encloses a wide and most romantic gorge. A succession of terraces for building-sites was formed on the hill-side, supported by massive walls (of rectangular, and in one or two instances of polygonal stones), large portions of which are still remaining. Directly back of the town rises a bold height of precipitous rock, with a cleft in the centre forming two peaks, facing the south, and called in ancient times the Phædriades, or "the Resplendent." These are the double-topped Parnassus of the poets, but in fact only a spur of the great mountain itself. At the foot of this cleft still issue the pure waters of the Castalian spring. An excavation in the rock, called the Bath of the Pythian Pilgrims, receives the stream, which flows thence down the sloping height to the wild glen below. The wall of rock by the spring's side is indented with artificial niches, large and small, for votive offerings. I drank (like a good Roman) nine draughts from the poetic fount, one for each Muse. Not far to the south from the Castalian spring are the remains of the Stadium; its outline can still be traced, and some rude seats in the rock at the upper extremity are preserved. Standing far up on the terraced height, it commands a delightful view of the Gulf, and of the wild picturesque gorge below the town. A little lower, near some tombs excavated in the rock, we enjoyed a charming prospect over the olive groves of the plain at the mouth of the romantic glen which Delphi overhangs, of Chryso and Galaxídi and Scala di Sálona, the bay, the gulf, and the mountains of the opposite shore of the Morea, among which Cyllene is conspicuous. Still lower down, in the pleasantly situated monastery of the Panagia, a few beautiful remains of ancient art are preserved; — a spirited and well-executed bas-relief, representing a chariot drawn by four noble horses towards an altar; a lion's head; fragments of bas-reliefs, architectural ornaments, triglyphs, and columns. In another monastery we saw a few old pillars and inscriptions, and on some stones near the site of the Pythian sanctuary are some very long and well-preserved inscriptions, which were discovered by Müller, and have been copied by the indefatigable German archæologists.

Still, as of old, the Muses of the poetic mountain use their witchery. The following song was written by my accomplished companion when fresh from their inspiration; its author's kindness enables me to give it to my readers. The Professor retains the modern popular orthography and accent, *Παρνασσό*.

A SONG OF PARNASSUS.

BY JOHN STUART BLACKIE.

On high Arachova's rocky slope
  The green vine richly grows;
From solemn Delphi's chasmed cliffs
  The pure fount largely flows.
Brightly, brightly beams the sea
  From Galaxidi's bay,
And brightly from the glowing pole
  Streams down the glorious day.
But me a soaring fancy lifts
  From this fair scene below,—

I 'll stride my jogging mule, and mount
  The lofty Parnassó!
          Ho! ho! ho!
          Ho! ho! ho!
        The lofty Parnassó.

Scramble, scramble o'er the ledge,
  And flounder o'er the stones!
Warily, warily, with sure foot
  Seize old Earth's giant bones!
Of Arab coursers I have read
  That breathe the fiery sun,
And steeds of golden English lords
  For golden cups that run;
But when from Delphi's rock-bound nook
  Aloft I wish to go,
I praise the stout, sure-footed mule
  That jogs to Parnassó.
          Ho! ho! ho! etc.

Now halt upon the lofty crag
  That rules the vale below;
'T is but the fringe of his huge robe
  Whose shoulder gleams with snow.
Look down upon the red-tiled huts
  In the low, corn-clad plain;
The ploughman's home thou shalt not see
  So near this night again.

Then up and down, and down and up,
  First right, then left, you go,
And when your joints are shaken well
  You 're nearer Parnassó.
        Ho! ho! ho! etc.

Wisely, wisely, like a ship
  When the strong northwester blew,
Softly, softly, like the wave
  That mounts a whirling screw, —
Thus my good mule the steep abreast
  Hath made a zigzag way,
Beneath the dark hosts of the pine
  That hide the gleaming day, —
Pines that feed upon the viewless
  Vapor of the snow,
Round the sides and up the back
  Of lofty Parnassó.
        Ho! ho! ho! etc.

The cuckoo sings, — the cuckoo's note
  How sweet in Parnassó!
And hark! the clear, low-tinkling bells
  Of sheep that wandering go.
And see! a little shepherd-boy,
  With shepherd's simple skill,
Perched sideways on his little mule,
  Comes piping up the hill.

Pipe away,! pipe away!
  Nightingales below!
Cuckoo, and pipe, and tinkling bells
  On lofty Parnassó!
                Ho! ho! ho! etc.

The shepherds built a leafy hut
  On lofty Parnassó,
And there they keep fresh cheese and milk
  High stored on Parnassó,
And eat, and drink, and watch their sheep,
  And keep a merry soul,
And when their flocks come home at eve,
  They swing upon a pole,
And laugh, and quaff, and tell old tales
  Beside bright fires that glow
Beneath the clear and dewless night
  Of lofty Parnassó!
                Ho! ho! ho! etc.

Shake down fresh branches of the pine,
  And we will make our bed
Where at our feet the dry logs blaze,
  And the stars shine overhead.
Ask not for quilted coverlet,
  Nor broidered curtains here;
This rough capote shall wrap thee round
  Till streaks of day appear.

So wise Ulysses slept of old,
  And great Achilles so;
So every lusty traveller now
  That 's fit for Parnassó.
    Ho! ho! ho! etc.

The twinklers of the night grow dim,
  The Borean sky is gray;
Come seize the path, my trusty mule,
  We 'll gain the top to-day.
Scramble, scramble up the ledge,
  And flounder o'er the stones;
Warily, warily, with sure feet
  Hold old Earth's giant bones!
Now thin and few, like locks of eld,
  The straggling pines do show,
And patches of white winter's robe
  Lie thick on Parnassó.
    Ho! ho! ho! etc.

Snow and stone, and stone and snow,
  Bare rock on rock all round:
But still a lovely bright blue flower
  You pluck from stony ground.
The little blue "Forget-me-not"
  With friendly face is seen,
And in snow-watered sunny nooks
  Shine spots of grassy green.

Blank high-peaked ridges stretching far
   A grisly rampart show;
But lightsome summer breezes kiss
   The peaks of Parnassó!
                                    Ho! ho! ho! etc.

Freely, freely, cast thine eye
   With raptured gaze around;
From peaks that cleave the skies behold
   Earth's various — pictured ground.
Lo where OLYMPUS hails the gods,
   And PINDUS cleaves the sky,
And where ZETOUNI'S waters round
   The high-souled Spartans lie.
From ACARNANIA'S craggy bound
   To steep MOREA'S snow,
Hills on hills and seas on seas
   Thou greet'st from Parnassó.
                                    Ho! ho! ho! etc.

Where green ZACYNTHUS' sunny isle
   With generous vintage glows;
Where from rich CORINTH'S mountain fort
   The mythic fountain flows;
Where famous ATHENS, girdled round
   With many a storied hill,
Her pillared wreck of chastest shrines
   Upholds serene and still,—

All lovely Greece before thee lies!
  Canst thou believe the show?
Bless God who brought thy pilgrim feet
  At length to Parnassó!
      Ho! ho! ho! etc.

The Roman and the Turk had swept
  For years this lovely land;
And many a grim old portal shows
  The Doge's stern command.
But now the land hath snapt her chain, —
  A slave she ne'er might be, —
And lovely Greece is free again,
  Mountain, and plain, and sea!
Canst thou believe the thing thou seest?
  Though freedom's growth be slow,
It grows, and ne'er shall die again,
  Round sacred Parnassó!
      Ho! ho! ho! etc.

Now fill this bowl with Santorin,
  That hopeful blood may glow,
While on my stout-paced mule again
  I wend down Parnassó.
Live Parnassó! live rock and pine,
  Green nook and bulwark gray,
The shepherds and the shepherds' hut,
  And sheep that tuneful stray!

Farewell, fair Mount! and evermore
  May vines for free Greeks grow
On high Aráchova's slopes that fringe
  The lofty Parnassó.
        Ho! ho! ho!
        Ho! ho! ho!
      The lofty Parnassó.

FROM DELPHI TO ATHENS.

What is the secret of the mighty influence which the Pythian oracle wielded for so many centuries throughout the Grecian world? Not, surely, mere vain superstition; not, as some of the Christian fathers imagined, the agency of evil spirits. Its true source, as Curtius has shown in his admirable History of Greece, is found in the intelligence, the knowledge, the wisdom, and the foresight of the Delphian priesthood. Careful watchers of the course of events in every province of Hellas and the whole ancient world, deep students of human nature, and inheriting profound maxims of practical wisdom from their predecessors, by the legitimate exercise of human faculties they were enabled to give the wisest counsel, and often to predict the issue of enterprises; while they had the cunning in doubtful cases to utter an ambiguous voice. Hence was it that

Delphi was the true centre of Greece, — the keystone of Grecian unity, the guide of Grecian activity.

As we rode out of Delphi in the morning, we stopped to examine some sarcophagi and tombs near the road on the hill-side, a little north of the town. We were particularly delighted with a sarcophagus of pure white marble, its sides adorned with bas-reliefs of exquisite finish; and the slab, which once formed the cover, and now lies near by, surmounted by a mutilated but exceedingly fine and lifelike statue of a female, in a recumbent posture. The sarcophagus has been broken in two, but the parts are preserved, and might easily be united, so as to leave little trace of the injury.

Along wild gorges, and through miles and miles of vineyards on the terraced hill-sides, we rode on to Aráchova. It is sad to think that the generous product of these luxuriant vines should be ruined, as it is every year, by the almost universal Greek custom of putting resin into the wine, imparting a flavour unendurable to a Frank, though acceptable to the taste of the natives. We tasted some of this vile compound at a khan in Aráchova, in which enough of the original excellence remained to show that it would be a wine of the rarest richness and deliciousness, had it not been spoiled by the resin. Our host, who offered us this wine, was a man of noble figure and classic features. It is probable that the old Greek blood has been preserved in much purity in the region of Parnassus; at any rate, the ancient type of face and form is often met with. At Aráchova, as at Kastri and several other villages in the neigbourhood, the tiles on the roofs are kept in place by stones placed upon them. The same custom prevails in some parts of Switzerland; and that it obtained in ancient Greece, also, there is reason to infer from the passage in Thucydides describing the attempted surprise of Platæa by a party of Thebans, in which the women and servants are represented as pelting the intruders with "stones and tiles" from the house-tops.

Through wild and picturesque glens, and grand gorges, we pursued our way hence,— the long, gray, bare rock of the heights of Parnassus in full view on the left. Among these mountain passes (not far from the Triple Way where Œdipus met his father Laius) we were overtaken by a brisk shower, — the first rain we had seen for a month in this cloudless land, — and we were well drenched when we arrived at our khan at Lebadea. As one approaches Lebadea from Parnassus, hills of an alluvial formation, with loose, fertile soil, take the place of the rock-ribbed mountains. This chain of arable hills extends nearly to Thebes.

The next morning, as we rode by the side of the Copaic "Lake," Nicolaos, one of our attendants, plucked long wreaths of beautiful and fragrant white clematis, which grows in great abundance and luxuriancy by the side of the path, and we twined them around our hats. We went, but by a different road, — along the roots of Helicon, and passing the noontide by the waters of a sacred fountain, — to our old khan at Eremókastri, and there spent the night. As we sat enjoying the beautiful view of the neighbouring mountains, bright-eyed Greek boys told us of Klephts descending from Helicon to a village which we saw, and murdering a peasant to obtain his property, and this but a month before. They talked, too, of their studies, at the excellent school in the village, and some of them offered ancient coins for sale.

To the battle-ground of Leuctra we rode the next morning; near it are the ruins of a Venetian tower. Thence to the plain of Platæa, — crossing the Asopus, muddy and sedgy, and riding through fields of yellow grain, enamelled with blue larkspurs, waving over the ancient scene of conflict. The site of the old city, on a gentle elevation rising from the plain, still exhibits extensive and interesting remains of walls and towers, built of large hewn blocks of limestone, considerably worn by time. The height of the remaining portion of the walls is, in general, but two or three courses. On higher ground, to the south, are remains of walls of the most ancient city. Some large, but coarse and rude sarcophagi, stand on the side of the hill.

In the house where we breakfasted, which contained but one apartment, its floor the ground, and with a long row of hens' nests near the fireplace, a boy, who had been to the schools in Thebes, showed us his little library, consisting of books of the Church, and several historical works, published by the American missionaries, and printed at the Greek press in Malta, about twenty years ago. My companion increased the young man's literary treasures by the present of a copy of a Greek translation of *Robinson Crusoe*, recently printed in Athens.*

Striking over the hills, along the sides of the long Mount Cithæron, at whose feet Platæa is built, we come at length into the road from Thebes to Athens, one of the few roads passable by carriages which Greece can boast. It is, on the whole, a very good road, but in some places so rough and stony as to subject the strength of a carriage to a severe test. On a

---

* No greater boon could be bestowed upon the Greeks than the translation into their language of some of the most wholesome works of English literature. The admirable version of the Pilgrim's Progress, published at Athens in 1854, is doubtless working good among them. "Poor Richard" might teach not unneeded lessons of practical wisdom; and, in higher fields, our language would afford much better aliment for their nascent civilization than the French, which at present, unfortunately, furnishes the larger portion of their intellectual food.

high hill, rising abruptly in the picturesque pass between Cithæron and Parnes, stand the high walls and towers of the acropolis of Œnoe. These are the best-preserved fortifications we saw in Greece; and their fortunate and commanding position adds to their imposing effect. In a guard-house, at the foot of the hill, we found a company of ten soldiers posted, and had a pleasant chat with their captain, who offered us resined wine. A little farther on, in the plain below, are the remains of a tower, supposed by some scholars to mark the site of Eleutheræ. An hour's ride hence brought us to a solitary khan, near a deserted church, on a moderate slope, overlooking a valley surrounded by green hills. A large tree, of the holly-oak, spread its shadow near the khan, and cool breezes offered their refreshment. Here we slept in the same room as the horses and mules, — a long apartment, its floor the earth. Near our beds our dinner was cooked, by a fire made on the ground, the smoke curling upwards, and finding its way out as it could through apertures in the blackened roof of tiles. In a long brick oven in the side-wall, large loaves of bread were baking; a goodly number of fowls sat on the nests, or perched at the side of the room near the horses, — cats and dogs prepared themselves for a night's rest, — and the servants stretched themselves out on their capotes, and soon were snoring around us.

The next morning, after a pleasant ride among the pine-dotted (rather than pine-clad) hills, we came to the large plain of Eleusis, by the side of the sea. Across the plain stretch the arches of a ruined aqueduct, built by the Romans. I had already visited Eleusis, making the excursion in a carriage from Athens, from which it is eleven miles distant; but it was delightful to see again the deep-blue waters of its bay, and the crags of Salamis. The greatest interest which attaches to Eleusis arises from its having been the seat of those august mysteries which gave men "sweeter hopes of a future life." The huts of the modern village are built near the site of the magnificent temple of Demeter. Fragments of columns of a large size, and of the most beautiful white marble, lie strewn around, and a few mutilated statues and sculptured reliefs are preserved in a rude little chapel; large foundation walls, also, are still perfect; but we found little else to testify to the splendour of the ancient edifice.*

The hill of the acropolis of Eleusis is long and low, but steep and rocky, and well adapted to its purpose. Remains of the old wall can still be traced upon it. From it there is a fine view of the plain and the sea, including the Rharian field, where Demeter is said to have first sown corn. We rested at a clean and comfortable khan, where Prof. Blackie amused an intelligent company of boys by ingeniously comparing the men of the most important countries in the world to different animals with similar characteristics.

Leaving the sacred city, we followed a most delightful path by the side of the exquisitely beautiful Gulf of Salamis, our prospect bounded by the brown and barren, but strikingly picturesque island. Nothing could be more unspeakably enchanting than those blue and

* Very extensive remains of the temple and of the propylæa have been discovered in the present year (1860), in the excavations undertaken by the French government.

historic waters, and the contrast between their intensely bright colour and the various hues of the rocky shores. Passing the sarcophagus and the ruins of the large monument of Strato, built of exquisite marble, we crossed the salt-springs, which of old formed the boundaries of the Athenians and Eleusinians, and soon came to the picturesque pass of Daphne. On the left are rocks indented with rudely-carved niches, and bearing inscriptions which show that the place was consecrated to Aphrodite. Near the end of the defile, at the highest point of the pass, and in one of the most delightful retreats in the neighbourhood of Athens, is the partially ruined monastery of Daphne, the burial-place of the Christian Dukes of Athens in the Middle Ages. Its church, of the Byzantine order, bears marks of injuries suffered from the Turks, in its blackened and mutilated walls and mosaics. In the centre of the dome is a large and quaint half-length figure, in mosaic, of our Saviour. Here, as in nearly all the old churches we visited in Greece, new pictures and furniture have been very recently added, by the munificence, generally, of Greek merchants residing abroad, or of Russians. A threefold picture, representing the death, ascension, and reception in heaven of the Virgin Mary, but just presented to the monastery, is admirable for the fine execution of many of its parts, and particularly the pure and deep expression of the faces, which are almost worthy of comparison with those of Frà Angelico; yet, as a whole, it has some of the Chinese-like stiffness characteristic of the pictures in Greek churches, which are still painted according to the traditions of the Byzantine school.

After enjoying, for the last time, the products of our cook's skill, in an excellent dinner, we turned our horses' heads towards Athens. We passed four dromedaries "all in a row," giving the scene something of an Oriental aspect. Never did the city of Athens appear more lovely than when we had gained the hills whence we looked down upon it. The whole plain, stretching from Pentelicus, between Parnes and Hymettus, to the sea, was spread out before us, the queen-like city in the centre, the graceful ruins on its acropolis transfigured by the last rays of the setting sun. The beautiful and picturesquely-outlined mountain of Pentelicus was all of a rich, dark purple, the long range of Hymettus was glowing in lilac tints, while the detached and romantic peak of Lycabettus, overhanging the city, shone yellow like burnished gold. The sea, calm and blue, stretched away in the distance, Ægina peered forth afar, and in the secure haven of the well-built town of the Peiræus rose the graceful masts of two American vessels of war, amidst the surrounding shipping, while the French fleet was distinctly visible near the entrance of the Gulf of Salamis. Along the old Sacred Way, by which the solemn processions moved to Eleusis, we rode, delighted by the beautiful scene; we crossed the bridge over the Cephissus, where the initiated, returning from the celebration of the mysteries, bandied jests with the Athenian populace; we passed the gardens of the Academy, and the site of the storied monuments of the Cerameicus; and soon warm grasps of the hand, and hearty salutations of friends, welcomed us back to Athens.

MARATHON.

"TAKE Herodotus and Byron," said Mr. Finlay, "for your guides to Marathon."

Aroused from short slumbers just after midnight on the morning of the 18th of June, at one o'clock I was astride the same good white horse that had carried me to Parnassus, and on my way, by the faint starlight, to the scene of the first great recorded victory of civilization over barbarism. Besides the admirable guides which Mr. Finlay recommended for the history of the battle, the scenery, and the sentiment, I needed a path-finder and a servant in human shape; and had engaged one skilled in his profession. He was taken, however, on this very night, with a Greek fever, caught in ascending Pentelicus in a hot sun the day before; but sent in his stead an intelligent young man from the "Seven Islands," whose best qualifications for his office were a plenty of good-nature, and a tolerable knowledge of English. I would gladly have exchanged the latter for a knowledge of the country. Passing the long, white, graceless palace of King Otho, built of limestone and stucco, and keeping the road near the banks of the Ilyssus till we had left Lycabettus behind us, as we rose to the great plain lying at the foot of the marble mountain, Pentelicus, and extending to the limerock sides of Hymettus on the one hand, and the winding ranges of Parnes on the other, a warm breeze saluted our cheeks, and drove away the chill of the lowlands. The thyme, and other aromatic herbs which clothe the plain, and feed the bees of Hymettus, filled the air with fragrance; and by and by, in the broadening light, the delicate blossoms of many varieties of flowers disclosed themselves, and the sweet matin songs of birds swelled upward around us. Little companies of peasants, — man, wife, and children, — riding on patient donkeys, or driving donkeys laden with panniers of vegetables or bundles of firewood, passed us on their way to market. A little to my surprise, the guide struck into a path to the right of Pentelicus, leading between that mountain and Hymettus; I knew, however, that, although the road to the left is the one pursued by travellers, there is a pass from the plain of Marathon, leaving the battle-field by the sea-side, and coming out between the two mountains; and congratulated myself that I was about to explore a comparatively unknown route. But at length we were told by some country people whom we met, that we could not reach Marathon by that path, and must retrace our steps and take the other road. My pretended "guide" thus showed himself no less ignorant (I afterwards found that he was much more ignorant) of the way than myself. Could I have spared another day for the excursion, I should have been inclined to push on and endeavour to reach the plain by this pass; but the danger of losing the way, or of being detained by obstacles such as marshes, thickets, and fences, and thus failing of reaching the battle-field altogether, induced me to prefer a certainty and take the beaten track.

And so we rode back, and came out between the two mountains, and then striking over the fields along the side of Pentelicus, now among little bushes, now over ploughed ground, and now in the deep, stony bed of a winter torrent, among high and gorgeous oleanders flushing its dry sands, came to the little village of Maroúsi, in the midst of olive-groves, where we found an old man standing in the yard in front of his cottage, and took him to guide us to the neighbouring town of Cephissia. After taking a cup of coffee in front of a little cafinet in the centre of the village, I rode on by rich gardens of fruit-trees, watered by rills from the Cephissus, and turned to visit the kephalári, or fountain, where this stream takes its rise. In a natural cavity, some ten or fifteen feet square, and about the same number of feet in depth, with its sides protected by a wall which may have sustained some ancient shrine built over the fount, the clear waters of the pure rivulet spring noiselessly from the ground, through the large clean stones which cover the bottom of the pool. The bright, transparent waters fill their well to the depth of about six feet, and then flow off in sparkling, leaping, silver, thread-like streamlets to fertilize the gardens of the most delightful villages of Attica. Cephissia is the summer retreat of the Athenian court, the foreign ambassadors, and the wealthier families. Its beautiful gardens are filled with fruit-trees in rich variety,— the olive, the fig, the pomegranate, the peach, the nectarine, the plum, the pear, and the walnut. In its delightful shades and waters, its greenness, and luxuriance of vegetation, it can hardly be less charming now than in the days of Herodes Atticus, of whose Cephissian villa Gellius speaks with such rapture. I breakfasted in this pleasant town. A noble old plane-tree, growing in the middle of a large square, into which the road had widened, spread its broad arms far and wide, and with its deep foliage cast a welcome shade from one side of the street to the other. Around its trunk is a level square, raised about a foot above the road, and protected by a border of stone; here there are a number of stone tables and benches, on which quiet citizens were sitting, discussing the news and speculating on the future glories of Greece, or partaking of coffee and spirits served from the rival shops on either side of the way. Under the beautiful leafy canopy I seated myself on one of the benches, and took the refreshment which my servant produced from his stores. It was nearly eight o'clock, and I found we had consumed five hours in wandering off the road; no pleasant thought, inasmuch as, even without any such accident, a journey to Marathon and back in the same day with the same horse is a hard one for both man and beast. We found here, however, an old man among the loiterers who said he was thoroughly acquainted with the road to Marathon, and the battle-field itself, with all the objects of interest to a stranger; he was a hale, active old fellow, although more than seventy winters had frosted his head, and I gladly hired him to guide us. So the old man, in his simple white sheep-skin raiment, trudged and trotted on before us, as brisk as a youth of twenty.

On the north side of Pentelicus, the prevailing rock in our path over the hill was mica-slate, with the strata upheaved at a large angle. Young pines grow luxuriantly on these hills, and a great variety of shrubs and flowers, among which I noticed the beautiful mist-tree, and the graceful and fragrant clematis. Passing, after a few hours, the little hamlet of Stamáta, from a hill-top we caught a glimpse of the beautiful sea and shore of Marathon, and saw, as we descended a mountain slope by a long, steep path, paved in part with slippery stones, the little village of Marathóna. Pushing on towards this village, we came upon a large meadow, at whose western end, on our left, stood a high round tower of mediæval date. Towards this the old Albanian began to run, pointing, gesticulating, and shouting, here was the battle fought; this was the ground that had drunk the blood of the Turks. "The Turks!" said I. "Pshaw! show me the field where your old Greeks routed the Persians." "The Persians?" — the old man had never heard of them; the name of Miltiades was equally strange to his ears; — so much for all his stories of guiding strangers to the immortal plain, all his boasts of familiarity with its localities. I explained the matter to my attendant, (for he knew no more of the history of Marathon than the old rustic,) and, in the first flush of vexation, we spurred our horses and galloped away from this profitless servant. We came soon to the banks of a little river (its course dry in the hot season), which, coming from among the hills, and washing the village of Marathóna, crosses the battle-field, and empties into the sea. On its side and in its bed rose countless oleanders of large size, with their glorious blossoms in their fullest beauty, — the finest specimens I saw even in Greece. By this flowery hedge we rode to the village, and, after inquiring of an intelligent citizen the proper way to the field, at once began to descend to it. We accosted some Albanian children playing near a well, but they did not understand modern Greek. Our path lay by the side of the river, or in its wide bed, covered with sand, and large, round, white marble stones.

Reaching the field, I saw at the distance of about three miles transversely, near the shore, the mound which covers the remains of the one hundred and ninety-two Athenians who fell in the battle; towards which we rode at once, thus crossing the middle of the plain.

No house or building of any kind rises in the broad field, but here and there cattle were grazing, and we rode over the stubble of corn newly reaped, or plunged through high standing grain, ripe and awaiting the sickle. The monument — simple, but more eloquent than the proudest trophies of brass or marble — was soon reached. It is a small tumulus, evidently artificial, and of light, crumbly soil. Its height is thirty feet, its circumference six hundred. A part of the mould has been removed or displaced, from curiosity to know its contents, in a considerable excavation at the top and on one side. Dry, pitiful grass, and a few thin, sickly bushes, are the mound's only covering; bushes so blighted and eaten by insects, that it was with the greatest difficulty I succeeded in finding any leaves upon them sufficiently uninjured to take with me as memorials. A few pebbles, gathered from the soil with which the dust of heroes has mingled, furnished more satisfactory mementos. From this mound, erected on the spot where was the thickest of the battle, — for the Athenians were buried where they fell, — I had an excellent view of the whole plain, and of the scene of the fight. A little more than half a mile distant is the shore; here the Persians landed, or a little farther to the south, near a marsh which forms a natural obstacle to egress from the field in that direction, and is covered with luxuriant reeds and rushes, and little shrubs. After lingering as long as the burning heat of the sun would allow, we turned to leave the field by another pass, which leads by the little hamlet of Vraná. Thus we rode across the site occupied by the camp of the Greeks, whether, as is generally supposed, it was pitched so as to cover this pass of Vraná, or whether, as Mr. Finlay argues, the line was inclined in another direction, so as to cover the pass to Athens near the sea.

In every part of the plain, and almost wherever I went in Greece, thistles grow in great numbers and variety, red, yellow, purple, and whitish-blue. Soon, along the wide, dry bed of a little river which flows into the field from the pass of Vraná, I found some oleanders with a profusion of gorgeous blossoms, and plucked large branches, from which, when

I halted for dinner, I selected little buds and flowers to press and keep.

A slight ascent brought us to a khan. A woman, with a group of ragged children, who lived in the lower rooms, was seated on the ground in front; but she could not give us the key to the travellers' room above. However, I ate my dinner on the steps, and then lay down on the broad upper stones and got a little sleep under the shade of its porch. Meanwhile my "guide," as he appeased his hunger at the foot of the stairs, was recounting, to the mistress of the house and an old man who had come up to see the strangers, the story of the glorious battle as he had heard it from my lips while we rode over the field together. His auditors, living as they did almost on the very ground of the battle, were as totally ignorant concerning it as he had been a few hours before!

I could allow little time for rest, and was soon ascending the high hill back of Vraná, but often stopping for a farewell look at the plain of immortal memories, which is nowhere seen to greater advantage than from these heights. In addition to its glorious associations, Marathon, with its high, embracing mountains, and its brilliant, beaming sea, is one of the loveliest pictures of natural scenery that earth can show. A long, low promontory, the Cynosura, whose gentle hills connect themselves with the stately mountains guarding the plain on the north, runs out into the sea with a most graceful curve, and with a beautiful beach, which, like that of the whole shore, is covered with sparkling white sand. West of this promontory is the marsh in which the greatest slaughter of the Persians occurred. Across the blue, bright waves, the island of Eubœa stretches far along in a continuous chain of hills and mountains of picturesque forms, and varied, ethereal colours. The field, in about half its length, lies facing this beautiful island; but in the southern part it looks out upon the broad open sea.

On our way homeward, a little before we reached Cephissia, we came up with the old man who had offered to guide us to the battle-field; he fell to crossing himself as soon as he saw us, protesting it was not his fault that he had not satisfied our wishes. I assured him I had not thought of letting him go uncompensated for his trouble, and was only waiting to get a piece of money changed at the village where I had expected to meet him. So, by and by, under that glorious plane-tree, I paid the old fellow, who, after all, was no more ignorant than some of his neighbours; and after a cup of coffee, and a pleasant chat with one of the accomplished Professors of the Athenian University, I set off for Athens.

I had watched the stars fading, one by one, in the early morning, as through gates of pearl the dawn approached, with her robes of saffron and her fingers of rose; and now they were again shining forth in the firmament, while the shades of night were falling around me. The drums were beating the nine o'clock tattoo in the Street of Æolus as, after a rapid ride, we entered the city, and it was twenty hours after we had set out in the morning when I dismounted at my hotel. The next day, when I rang for breakfast, my landlady asked me whether I would have my soup or my coffee. It was nearly three o'clock, and past my usual dinner-hour. When I told my friends of my journey, they congratulated me on these prolonged slumbers; for without them, after so fatiguing a ride on a day when the Sun Demon raged with unusual violence, I could hardly have escaped without the terrible penalty of a Greek fever.

THE RUINS OF ATHENS.

"Earth proudly wears the Parthenon,
As the best gem upon her zone.
. . . . .
For out of Thought's interior sphere
These wonders rose to upper air;
And Nature gladly gave them place,
Adopted them into her race,
And granted them an equal date
With Andes and with Ararat."

EMERSON.

If you stand in the Street of Æolus, the principal street of modern Athens, you see at its southern end the bold crag of the Acropolis, crowned by the graceful ruins of the Erechtheum and the Parthenon. To this, the centre of all interest, whether we regard the history of Athens, her religion, or her art, let us turn our steps.

At the end of the street, just where the slope begins which leads up to the foot of the long rocky height, we find an octagonal tower of marble, built about a hundred years before our era, — the Horologe of Andronicus Cyrrhestes. It is commonly called the Tower of the Winds, its sides facing respectively the eight principal points of the compass, which are marked by the figures of the winds from those points, sculptured on the frieze, and represented in rapid flight, — the more rude and boisterous as males, the milder as females. The figures are still in good preservation, except some mutilation of the faces, (the Turks made it a point of religion to disfigure graven images, particularly by knocking off the noses), and well exhibit the character of the different winds. A bronze Triton on the top used to serve as a weathercock; and the time of day was indicated by sun-dials on the outside, or, in cloudy weather, by a water-clock in the interior. The Triton is gone, and the clepsydra; but the indexes of the sun-dials have been recently renewed. On the south side, a few feet from the tower, are two massive arches, a part of the aqueduct which conducted water to the clock. These arches have been recently excavated; and, as the earth has been removed around the tower, the whole building stands fifteen or twenty feet below the present surface of the neighbouring ground, which has been raised by the accumulation of soil and the *débris* of ancient structures.

If we are impatient to stand before the Parthenon, we ought, starting from this point, to wind around the hill to the right; but we will take the path on the left, as we shall thus find more objects of interest on our way. The brown wall of the Acropolis, rising from the edge of the cliff, contains remains of the old Hellenic wall, but is made up for the most part of the rude constructions of mediæval and Turkish times. Fragments of white marble, the wrecks, perhaps, of cunning workmanship, gleam now and then from among its irregular stones. In the north wall, which we are facing as we stand by the horologe, we find occasionally large parallelogram blocks, and some twenty-six drums of columns, together with architrave-stones. These very interesting relics are probably from the original temple on the site of the Parthenon, which was burned by the Persians, — its ruins affording ready material for Themistocles when he hastily rebuilt the walls of the citadel.

Winding around and up the hill, among low, wretched hovels, whose rude walls boast fragments, now and then, of ancient marbles, sometimes finely sculptured, we soon stand on the site of the Street of the Tripods. This street was lined by the little monuments or chapels erected by the leaders in the dramatic choruses, to receive and display the bronze tripods given as prizes for the success of the choruses whose expenses they had defrayed. The tripods were consecrated to Dionysus, the god in whose honour the dramatic festivals were held. Of these structures one lovely example remains, — the Chorēgic Monument of Lysicrates, erected B. C. 335. It is a little circular structure, thirty-five feet in height, with six Corinthian columns; and its roof is crested by an exquisitely beautiful finial (designed as a pedestal for the tripod), which swells upwards in graceful shape, and curves with plume-like drooping at the three corners of its triangular summit. The spirited frieze represents Dionysus and his attendant satyrs turning the Tyrrhenian pirates into dolphins. The metamorphosis in some places is but half completed, so that human legs are striking out from dolphins' bodies. These sculptures, as well as the columns and the finial, are considerably mutilated; but for all that the monument is still a little gem.

We are now turning the southeast corner of the citadel, and as soon as we have fairly reached the southern side, we are on the site of the renowned Theatre of Dionysus. The outlines of the theatre and a few of its rows of seats are all that can now be traced; yet what delight in standing on the very spot which witnessed the triumphs of Æschylus, Sophocles, Euripides, and Aristophanes! A little grotto in the rock, just above the theatre, was formerly adorned with statues, and is still surmounted by two columns of unequal height, reared to support consecrated tripods which had been obtained as chorēgic prizes. Passing on through the ruins of some arches, of uncertain history, we come to the extensive remains of the Odeum, or Music

Theatre, built by the munificent Herodes Atticus in the time of Marcus Aurelius. They are in the Roman style, and have no beauty to detain us long.

We are at the southwest corner of the Acropolis, and near the entrance to the citadel. Imagine a rocky height, rising precipitously * from the plain, so as to be inaccessible on all sides but the west, where it is approached by a gentle slope; give it an elevation of three hundred and fifty feet above the vale of Athens, and five hundred and sixty-nine above the sea, a length of about nine hundred and fifty feet from east to west, and a breadth of four hundred and thirty from north to south. This is the Acropolis. Its summit was levelled, probably by the early Pelasgian inhabitants, who made their abode upon this rock. The site of the first settlement, the fortress of the city, the oldest and most sacred seat of the gods, the consecrated pedestal which upbore

* The sides of the rock originally rose almost perpendicularly; but the *débris* of ancient ruins, thrown down from above, decreases at present their apparent height.

the most glorious works of Athenian art, in architecture, sculpture, and painting: — enter with reverence, for thou art ascending to the Athens of Athens, the Greece of Greece!

Unsightly mediæval and Turkish walls are drawn to shelter the western approach. Removing their rude stones, a few months before my visit, a French gentleman disclosed a Doric gateway, facing the Propylæa, and very likely the ancient entrance. But, as this gateway is blocked up, the only admission within the citadel is by a little door at the southwest corner. We enter a yard, where, in the marble fragments of old edifices and statues piled around in rich profusion, we have a foretaste of the scene of costly ruin which the whole hill presents. A soldier comes forward to take the card of admission which we have obtained, by paying a small fee, from M. Pittákys, the Inspector of Antiquities; another soldier accompanies us over the citadel, to see that we remove no fragment of ancient workmanship. A slight turn, and at our right, crowning a high, tower-like projection of the Cimonian wall, rises a very small, but exquisitely beautiful temple, that of the Wingless Victory,*—Victory who would never desert that people in whose fortress and among whose gods she had taken up her abode. Four graceful Ionic columns on each front sustain the pediment, and a highly ornamented frieze, portions of which remain, surrounded the building. A balustrade of marble slabs, adorned with exquisite reliefs, ran along the northern edge of the wall on which the temple stands, to guard the narrow passage-way; some of these slabs are now preserved in the interior of the building, one of which, representing Victory unloosing her sandals, is of singular beauty, spirit, and grace. The recent history of the temple is interesting. It was seen in 1676 by the travellers Spon and Wheler; but a century ago it had entirely disappeared. In 1835, however, in some excavations among the ruins of a Turkish bastion, carried on by the German archæologist, Ross, its fragments were discovered, and with great skill restored to their original position.

* This temple of Νίκη ἄπτερος "is only twenty-seven feet long, eighteen feet broad, and, from the lowest step to the top of the pediment, not more than twenty-three feet high."

To gain the temple of Victory, we ascended the noble flight of steps which led up from the Agora to the Propylæa. It was paved in the middle with slabs furrowed crosswise for the horsemen, and furnished at the sides with steps of marble, of which only broken and interrupted fragments remain. We are facing the ruins of that noble gateway — the Propylæa — which Pericles built, B. C. 437–432, with a magnificence worthy of the architectural glories to which it is the prelude. Let us before our mind's eye restore the structure in its original perfection. It was the problem of the architect to combine a cheerful "overture" to the Parthenon and other temples of the Acropolis, with the strength of the entrance to a fortress; and in this he happily succeeded. A broad portico of six Doric columns in the centre, with a wider interval between the two middle columns than the rest, invites us to enter; on either flank boldly project two marble halls or chambers, (the northern a picture-gallery, the southern an arsenal,) entered each through a portico of three columns on the side adjacent to the central structure, but presenting a line of strong and solid wall on their western faces, towards the approaching visitor; while the military character of the edifice was still further indicated by the projection of the Cimonian wall, (crowned by the little temple of the Wingless Victory,) which forms a solid tower directly in front of the arsenal, and stands on the right of the flight of steps, according to the law in Greek fortification, so as to take an approaching enemy on the side unprotected by his shield. On reaching the portico, you find that it introduces you to a hall, covered with a marble roof, which has a depth of forty-three feet, and is terminated by a solid marble wall, pierced with five gateways diminishing in height from the central and wider to the two outmost. The middle and wider passage-way within this hall is flanked by three Ionic columns on each side. The happy interchange of the Doric and Ionic orders, the graceful proportions of the whole structure, the exquisite carvings and brilliant colours of the roof, the wealth of statues, bronzes, and votive offerings with which the hall was adorned, combined to render the Propylæa one of the most glorious creations even of the age of Pericles, and the envy of Greece. Nor could the spirit of the Athenians be better symbolized, or the double purpose of the structure itself better indicated, than by the dedication of the two apartments on either side of the central portico to Art and to Arms, — the Pinacotheca, on the north, being filled with master-pieces of the first painters of the age, and the southern chamber being occupied as an arsenal. The doors with which the five gateways were closed were of wood, but elaborately carved and heavily gilded. Passing through them, the visitor found himself in another portico, of little depth, formed by six Doric columns precisely corresponding with those of the western front, through which he saw the statue of Athena Promachos, the peerless Parthenon, and the other wonders of the storied hill.*

* The central part of the Propylæa is most simply described as a wall, pierced with five gates, and enclosed within a double portico. It was fifty-eight feet in breadth; the

But of this magnificent structure the modern traveller finds only a shattered wreck. It is well that he should be prepared at once for the desolation and ruin which mar the reliques of the Parthenon, that his eye, recovered from the first shock of disappointment and sorrow, may dwell the more lovingly upon the inimitable grace and beauty which assert their immortality in the midst of all this decay. In place of the arsenal, now rises a tall, unsightly tower, built by a Frankish duke in the fifteenth century. The roofs and pediments of the central structure and of the Pinacotheca have vanished; while most of the columns of the western portico, and all the Ionic columns of the pillared corridor behind them, have lost their capitals, and remain but in about three fourths of their origi-

---

western portico forty-three feet in depth, the eastern some twenty feet. The Doric columns were four and a half feet in diameter and nearly twenty-nine feet in height. The two wings projected twenty-six feet in front of the central structure; the picture-gallery, entered through a porch twelve feet in depth, was itself thirty-five feet by thirty, the arsenal twenty-six by seventeen.

nal height.* Yet still are these rich marble walls and swelling columns irresistibly winning, still do they extort a tribute of admiration from the pilgrim who is hastening beyond.

On every side, in the Pinacotheca and central hall of the Propylæa, we have seen piled fragments of ancient statues, friezes, soffits, and other architectural ornaments, and similar heaps of shattered splendour meet us on our way to the Parthenon. That loveliest of

* Of the Pinacotheca the walls are nearly perfect, and the three Doric columns entire. The two columns at either end of the western portico are well preserved, but the four others mutilated as I have described; the eastern portico retains its six columns in tolerable preservation, although the blocks of which they are composed are considerably mutilated, and the capital of one of them lies broken at its feet.

I was interested in the proof of the unfinished state in which the Propylæa was left (the disastrous Peloponnesian war breaking out before it was entirely completed) furnished by the bosses or projections from the centre of the marble blocks in a part of the inner wall. Those which I first saw were so regular, that I thought they might have been intended as ornaments, to relieve the blankness of the wall; but a little further examination showed that this explanation is inadmissible, and that they were left to facilitate the raising of the blocks, with the intention of removing them and smoothing the stones after the walls had been erected.

temples stood on the highest part of the hill, — on ground forty feet higher than the Propylæa, — and not directly in front of this gateway, but at a considerable angle to the right, as the Greeks liked to approach their temples. Its western façade rises boldly before us, nor shall we soon have eyes for anything else.

Yet in the days of Athenian glory this peerless edifice was but one — though indeed the noblest — in the multitude of stately structures borne by the sacred hill. Shrines, temples, and statues of gods, heroes, and illustrious men, were crowded together on the hallowed ground. One of the foremost and most impressive inhabitants of this chosen home of religion and art was Athena Promachos, — Athena the Champion of the City, — whose colossal statue of bronze, wrought by the cunning hand of Phidias, bearing lance and shield, and clad with ægis and helmet, rose to the height of upwards of seventy feet, keeping watch and ward over the sanctuaries and the fortress of her favourite city. Her gilded spear-point, glittering above the roofs of the Parthenon, was visible off the Cape of

Sunium to the mariner approaching Athens. Pagan superstition believed the legend that Alaric, when at the end of the fourth century he came to Athens bent upon conquest and pillage, was stricken with superstitious terrour as he beheld the stately image of the warlike goddess towering above the citadel, and withdrew without molesting the people she guarded.

The path to the Parthenon led to the east, passing along the northern side of the building, and between it and the statue of Athena Promachos. The entrance to the Greek temples was almost always on the east. It was not the object of these edifices to accommodate a throng of worshippers; but they were built as houses for the gods, not for men,— as shrines in which the sacred image should dwell securely, and which should be of a magnificence and beauty worthy of their indweller. They were elevated upon platforms above the surrounding ground, so as to stand out from all profane structures as something apart; and the peristyle was raised three steps above these platforms, that he who entered might come with the good omen of having struck both the first and the last step with his right foot. The statue of the god was placed in the cella, or chief apartment of the temple, which, in accordance with its design of sheltering the image and separating it from everything profane, was enclosed by solid walls; but not on the east,—for here, in front of the temple, stood the altar of burnt offerings, and the suppliant would fain offer his sacrifice in sight of the god. Accordingly, on this side a wide doorway was left open, behind the vestibule, which was formed by a row of columns standing opposite to those of the exterior portico, and met at each end by an extension of the side walls of the cella.

The Parthenon, as the name implies, was the "House of the Virgin,"—the fane of the maiden goddess Athena. Its solid walls of Pentelic marble were surrounded by an ambulatory of forty-six Doric columns, eight on each end and seventeen on each side (counting the two exterior columns twice). After ascending the three steps which conduct the visitor to the floor of the eastern portico, he mounts two more steps to enter the vestibule or pronaos. Six Doric columns mark the outer limit of this vestibule, and the interstices between them were filled by a gilded grating. Within the pronaos stood the golden basin of water for purification, while votive gifts of various kinds were suspended on the walls or borne by tripods and tables. The wall itself was painted.

The cella proper, entered from this porch, contained the magnificent statue of Athena, by Phidias, made of ivory and gold. The apartment itself was nearly a hundred feet long, and above sixty feet in width. Two ranges of pillars, one above the other, supported the roof, — for the temple was hypæthral (that is to say, lighted from above), and the aperture to admit the light made such support necessary. The aperture had a movable covering of bronze, and was open only on days of festival; at such times, from the clear blue heavens, the light fell in the most advantageous way upon the colossal statue, which stood below, upon a platform of Piræan tufa, not immediately beneath, but a little beyond the opening in the roof. "This plastic hymn, celebrating the might and greatness of the goddess," is thus described by Hettner: "A long garment falls in massive and graceful folds to her feet, and is enriched at the breast with an ivory mask of Medusa; the head is covered by a helmet, on the top of which rests a sphinx, and on each side a griffin, carved in relief. In her left hand she bears a spear, round which twines the sacred snake of the citadel; in her right, Nikē, the golden goddess of victory; at her feet leans her shield. On the base of the statue is represented the birth of Pandora; along the edge of her sandals, the victory over the Centaurs; and on her shield, her other conquests, — outside, the battle with the Amazons, — inside, the conflict with the giants." * In the inner chamber, formed by the pillars surrounding the statue, which were connected with each other, perhaps, by gratings, — the Parthenon proper, in the stricter sense, — were placed the no-

* The statue was thirty-nine feet seven inches in height, the figure of Victory six feet high.

blest and most beautiful gifts presented to the shrine.

Behind the cella was another apartment, separated from it by a solid wall, and entered only from the west, — the Opisthodomus. This was the Treasury of the temple and of the state. Its walls were painted by Polygnotus. Four pillars supported the ceiling, "which, as in other temples, was painted with golden stars on a blue ground, in imitation of the open sky." It was entered through a pronaos or porch, precisely corresponding with that of the eastern end.

More wondrous even than the exquisite proportions of the building itself, and the effect of majesty and grace which it produced, were the sculptures with which its exterior was profusely adorned. The mutilated statue of Theseus (as it is called in England, many German scholars dissenting), from the pediment of the Parthenon, is justly regarded as the finest statue in the world; and, altogether, in pediments, metopes, and frieze, the Fane of the Virgin was decked with the very highest and noblest works in sculpture to which human genius ever gave birth. The figures of the pedimental sculptures — not less than twenty to twenty-five in number in each pediment — were full and complete, detached from the wall, and, like all the works of Phidias, finished *ad unguem*, even in the parts entirely removed from the sight of the visitor:

"For the gods see everywhere."

Those of the eastern front represented the birth of Athena, and her reception in the assembly of the gods; the western, the victory of the goddess in her contest with Poseidon for the land of Attica. The sculptured metopes — ninety-two in all — filled the intervals between the triglyphs in the frieze of the peristyle. They represented, in very bold relief (parts of the figures being quite detached from the tablets), various incidents in the life of Athena, exploits of her favorite heroes, and combats with centaurs. And the entire wall of the cella, within the peristyle, was surrounded by a sculptured frieze, in a continuous line of bas-reliefs five hundred and twenty-four feet in length, representing the joyous procession of the great Panathenaic festival, which carried the *peplos*, or sacred veil, wrought annually by the maidens of Athens, and other gifts for the goddess, to her sanctuary. This frieze is as admirable in its way as the pedimental sculptures in theirs, — the highest achievement of art in this kind. The life, the grace, the variety of the figures, — the perfect representation, in their different characters, of grave old men, spirited youth, and winning maidens, — the horses, which, as Flaxman says (in words often quoted, because so true), "appear to live and move, to roll their eyes, to gallop, prance, and curvet," — command the admiration of the world. How easily and gracefully sit those horsemen, — what life and reality in every group! I once visited the imperial stud at Tarbes, in France, when a party of soldiers were riding some twenty or thirty noble animals of the purest Arabian and English blood, for exercise, in the field. The horses were full of fire, and life, and frolic; I exclaimed at once, "It is the frieze of the Parthenon realized!" and I felt, as I had never felt before, the full power and genius of those old Greek sculptors.

Such were the adornments of the Virgin's Fane, — so lovely, that, when we contemplate them alone, the whole edifice, so exquisitely symmetrical, seems but the pedestal which supported those wondrous sculptures, — the casket which enshrined that matchless statue. But in the construction of the temple itself there are hidden refinements and delicacies which testify no less strikingly to the genius of the builders. Its architects had caught from Nature her cunning secret of avoiding straight lines by delicate curves. Thus every apparently horizontal line in the building — as in the upper surfaces of the steps, the entablature, etc. — rises at the centre in an almost imperceptible curve from either end; the columns, as they gently taper upwards, swell with a hyperbolic entasis; while vertical lines are equally avoided, the columns inclining slightly towards the centre of the building, and the walls themselves inclining inwards, so that every apparently vertical line produced would meet in one point, —

of course at an immense distance above the building. The curves are conic sections, wrought out with extreme accuracy and subtilty of reference to the optical effect. I doubt not that the exquisite eye of the Greeks, so sensitive to beauty, first taught them to employ these delicate curves; and that they afterwards applied their admirable mathematical science to the development of the laws by which their use should be governed. While beauty and grace are heightened by these nice deviations from rectilineal structure, the effect of the absence of perpendicularity, or the slight approach to the pyramidal form, is strength and repose.

It is true that one object of the curves is to correct the optical illusion by which a horizontal line perfectly straight appears to sag, and a column tapering regularly to be depressed in the middle; as intelligent builders raise the king-post an inch or two higher than the other supports of a roof, knowing that the ridge must be slightly elevated in the centre to appear horizontal. But the swell in the lines of the Parthenon is more than corrective; though almost imperceptible, it is just sufficient to add a mysterious grace and softness to the contour, and constitute one of those peculiar charms, always felt though till lately inexplicable, the absence of which in all the modern imitations of classical architecture makes them comparatively so cold and harsh. I could distinctly trace the swell in the columns, and thought I could perceive the curves in other lines of the temple; and yet they are so delicate that no one would detect them, were he not previously aware of their existence; and, although they were noticed by Vitruvius, the modern world has been strangely ignorant in the matter, until the recent investigations of Pennethorne and Penrose.*

Moreover, to all the perfect graces of form there were added here the richest enchantments of colour. For that in the Parthenon,

* In a visit to the Acropolis, one evening, I satisfied some sceptical companions of the existence of this curve on the upper step of the Parthenon, by getting one of them to hold a lighted match at one end while his friend at the other end looked along the surface of the step. It was not until the match had been raised some six inches above the marble that it became visible from the other end.

as in ancient temples generally, the architectural effect was heightened by painting, there is no longer room for doubt. The wall of the tympanum was coloured, to bring out the pedimental statues in bolder relief. There are indications that the cornice was decorated with "painted ovoli and arrows, coloured meanders, and honeysuckle ornaments," and that gilded festoons hung on the architraves, below the triglyphs, which, as well as the guttæ, were painted azure. The ceilings were painted in blue and gold; and, besides these colours, ochre and vermilion were used in the decorations. The drapery of the figures on the frieze was marked with colour and gilding, but the human form stood out in the white purity of marble. And that the shafts of the pillars, and the walls of the temple, were not coloured, is the best established opinion. To add pigments to the broad masses of that rich Pentelic marble would be indeed "to paint the lily;" although the walls of temples of inferior stone, covered with stucco, needed and received such embellishment. It is still maintained by some, however, that the whole surface was stained with ochre or other pigment; for what purpose I know not, unless to soften the dazzling brilliancy of the marble. The question is one of fact, as well as of *a priori* probability; and we find, that, while the traces of colouring in the parts already alluded to have been so clearly ascertained as to be admitted on all hands, no colour has been detected on the outer cella-walls and pillar-shafts of the marble temples of Athens, except such as receives its most natural explanation in the effect of oxidation, and the growth of mosses or other vegetable matter. But to whatever extent the painting of the temple was carried, it must have been controlled by the same exquisite taste as was displayed in every other feature of the building.

Less than two hundred years ago this wondrous structure survived, almost uninjured by time. The chryselephantine statue of Athena had been carried to Constantinople; her shrine had been converted, successively, into a Christian church — first of the "Divine Wisdom," or the Word, afterwards of the Virgin Mary —

and a Mohammedan mosque. Yet were the walls unbroken, the splendours of pediments, frieze, and metopes little impaired. The bombardment of the Acropolis by the Venetians in 1687 dashed the middle of the Parthenon to pieces; Morosini, the Venetian commander, broke some of the noblest statues of the pediment to atoms in an unskilful attempt to remove them; and in more recent times the work of spoliation was continued by Lord Elgin. And now at first sight the visitor is oppressed by the mournful aspect of ruin,— at least if, as in my case, he has received from drawings the impression of less mutilation than exists in fact. The roof is gone, and the whole centre of the building thrown down; fourteen columns of the peristyle, on the north and south, and five of the eastern vestibule, have been prostrated, and all the columns and division-walls of the interior apartments destroyed. But the majesty, and grace, and beauty, which, after all the havoc, still speak in these stones, throw an irresistible spell around you, and you hardly miss what is absent, just as you never feel the want of the arms when you look at that victorious Venus, who once looked down in proud beauty upon the thronged theatre of Melos, and still conquers all hearts as of yore.

There was no barbaric splendour about the architectural wonders of Athens; it was not to stupendous size, or profusion of costly ornament, that they owed their effect; in all things, the Athenians knew how to unite beauty with simplicity.* The Parthenon is of moderate dimensions, — two hundred and twenty-eight feet in length, one hundred and one in breadth, and sixty-six in height to the top of the pediments (omitting fractions); † and yet, both at my first and every subsequent visit, I was struck with its majesty, as well as its grace. But its great charm is the perfect harmony which breathes in it, — the cheerfulness, the serenity, which reign in its

---

* Φιλοκαλοῦμεν γὰρ μετ' εὐτελείας. — Funeral Oration of Pericles, Thucyd. II. 40.

† In *mere size* the Parthenon is far surpassed by Girard College, — one of the noblest modern buildings in the Grecian style. The latter has a length of two hundred and eighteen feet, a breadth of one hundred and sixty, and a height of ninety-seven feet.

lovely proportions. It dwells in immortal calm, enthroned in that pure and serene beauty which is the type of the highest excellence in human character, — the complete symmetry of mind and heart and will, under the supreme control of true religion. I do not mean that this symbolic significance is due to any conscious purpose of the architects, any more than I believe that the builders of Gothic cathedrals intended to symbolize the mystery and aspiration of Christian faith. "They builded better than they knew;" and one of the noblest vindications of art lies in the fact that there are meanings and relations in all beauty, which correspond to every truth.

The world is apt to regard with some suspicion rhapsodies over the great works of classical art and literature. But although it be true that among the admirers of antiquity, as in every other class of persons, you may find some extravagant enthusiasts, all men of catholic taste and cultivation, of whatever school, unite in paying homage to the architects and sculptors of Athens. Genius is not confined to one race or one epoch. The memory of the Parthenon but heightened the admiration and reverence with which I floated along the watery streets of Venice, or stood beneath the dome of St. Peter's; paced the grand nave of Milan, or climbed the towers and galleries of Amiens, Rouen, Strasburg, and Cologne. New times and new institutions must give rise to new styles of architecture, fitted to their peculiar demands. It would be absurd to take an idol-house of the Greeks as the model for the place of worship of a Christian congregation. True taste is bound in the trammels of no narrow partisanship; heirs as we are of all the ages, let us admire and be grateful for our richly varied inheritance in the monuments of classic, mediæval, and modern times. But in complete grace and symmetry and harmony, in wondrous delicacy and learned refinement of construction, in the association of the highest achievements of sculpture, what building in the world is the peer of the Parthenon?

As you admire an exquisite ode of Simonides, though fresh from the stately epic of Homer, even so when you turn from the splendours of the Virgin's Fane does the graceful ruin of the Erechtheum delight you. Without the majesty of its stately neighbour, it breathes an exquisite grace and a winning loveliness unrivalled. Nowhere else has Greek architecture so well displayed its powers of adaptation. Here were a number of sacred objects, irregularly placed, which were to be comprehended within one structure, properly distributed, at the same time, in their appropriate apartments: the olive-tree which sprang up at Athena's bidding, — the salt spring which burst forth at the touch of Poseidon's trident, — the ancient altars of various gods and national heroes, — the graves of Cecrops, Erechtheus, and Butes, — the lair of the sacred serpent, — the sanctuary of Pandrosus, — and above all the fane of Athena Polias, whose statue of olive-wood, the most venerable object of worship in Athens, was reputed to have fallen from heaven. To her was allotted the largest section of the temple, entered from the eastern portico; while behind it was the Pandroseum, with its portico on the north. These two cellæ filled the main body of the building, which is thirty-seven feet in breadth and seventy-three feet in length. Before the statue of Athena burned a golden lamp, both night and day, furnished with a wick of asbestos, and fed with oil once a year; a brazen palm-tree, rising above it to the roof, carried off the smoke. Persian spoils, — as the silver-footed throne on which Xerxes sat, upon

> "the rocky brow
> Which looks o'er sea-born Salamis,"

and the sword of Mardonius, taken at Platæa, — a folding-chair made by Dædalus, — and a wooden Hermes said to have been presented by Cecrops, — were among the objects whose presence filled the shrine with interesting associations.

The six Ionic columns of the northern portico, and five of the six of the eastern, are still standing. The northern is the larger and the nobler; it stands on ground eight feet lower than the other, — hence its columns are higher. The intercolumnar distances, also, here are greater ;* and the whole portico has a lightness and gracefulness which make it the most charming example of the Ionic order in the world. The neck of the shafts, below the capitals, is exquisitely adorned with flowers and leafage, — a prophecy of the Corinthian capital, to which the Ionic subsequently gave birth. All the mouldings and ornaments of the entablature, and the arabesques of the doorways, are singularly lovely and elegant.

At the western end, the wall rose unbroken to about half the height of the building, where it is surmounted by four Ionic pillars, whose interspaces were either left open, or closed with some transparent material. The effect of these novel windows is very beautiful ; and the significance of the construction lies herein, that the eastern portico would

---

* The height of the pillars in the eastern portico is eight and three fifths diameters ; in the northern, nine and a half ; — the distance of the pillars from each other is two diameters in the former, three in the latter ; — the height of the entablature on the eastern portico, two and one ninth diameters ; on the northern, only two.

lead you to expect a corresponding portico at the western end, while from the fact that the Pandroseum occupies, transversely, the western part of the building, such a portico, projecting from its side wall, would be an architectural absurdity. The present arrangement reconciles conflicting demands, by its felicitous intermingling of wall and pillars.

But the most unique feature of the Erechtheum is the southern portico. Six Athenian maidens, carved in marble, of colossal size, upbear the entablature, — I do not say the roof, for the portico (or, rather, sacred enclosure) stood open to the sky. They are clad in the robes worn by the virgins in the Panathenaic procession. Of grand and noble forms, serene and stately, firmly, but without effort, they bear the load imposed, while in their whole attitude, and in every feature of their lovely faces, reign a grace and a sweetness ineffably winning. There was probably some special propriety, resulting from the religious associations of the place, which justified the architect in his bold, but most successful, use of the human form as an architectural member. How different the effortless ease of these noble maidens from the contortions and agonies of the monstrous Caryatides and Atlantes of the Renaissance! One of these statue-pillars was carried to London by Lord Elgin; its place has been recently supplied by a wooden effigy, and the entablature replaced. Within this roofless enclosure, it is supposed, grew the sacred olive-tree.

The frieze of the Erechtheum was adorned with exquisite sculptures representing some festive procession; but of them we have but few and mutilated remains. The name of "the house of Erechtheus" was given to this assemblage of shrines from the mythic builder of the old temple, which occupied the same site, and was (itself or its successor) burned by Xerxes. The present structure was built a little after the Parthenon and Propylæa, — begun, perhaps, under Pericles, but not completed till about the year 393 B. C. Time has shattered and defaced the lovely temple; the Moslem lords of Athens converted it into a harem; but the charm of its original loveliness could not be wholly destroyed, and the world can hardly show a structure more captivating in its beautiful harmony.

We must not forget the great distinction between the Erechtheum and the Parthenon, which Boetticher and Curtius have recently pointed out, that, while the former was a temple for worship, — the most holy sanctuary of the city, with its priests, its sacrifices, and its perpetual flame, — the latter, built in honour of the goddess rather than for her immediate service, had a political as well as a religious significance, and symbolized the glory at once of Athens and of Athena. In form, it is true, the Parthenon was a temple; and its chryselephantine statue, though not directly an object of worship, was the most impressive revelation of the divine attributes of the goddess, the most glorious offering consecrated in her name. While the ancient, misshapen idol of Athena Polias, said to have fallen from heaven, was venerated with profound and superstitious awe, the magnificent image wrought by Phidias received a more intellectual homage. Worthily did she preside over the select assemblage collected within the Parthenon, when the judges, sitting at her feet, bestowed the prizes upon the victors in the great Panathenaic festival; but this was probably the only occasion when her sanctuary was employed for a public purpose.* As for the Opisthodomus, the purpose for which it was occupied was directly secular; yet it was quite in character with the religious spirit of the Athenians to invoke the protec-

* Curtius — whose learning and fine æsthetic sense have done so much to illustrate the monuments of Athens — has noticed the concentration in the Parthenon of symbols of that emulation "which was the soul of the Periclean state." "Here belong," he says, "not only the image of Nikē, which sprang from the hand of the Parthenos to meet the victors, but also the prize-vases on the top of the temple and the shields on its architrave. The pediments represented Athena herself as the resplendent and victorious goddess in heaven and upon the earth; in the metopes the heroes are presented in victorious combats, in the frieze the Athenians, as the foremost of the Greeks." — Gr. Gesch., II. 275.

I have already called attention (North American Review, Oct., 1858, Article VIII.) to the admirable work from which I make this quotation. The second volume, recently published, amply fulfils the promise of the first. No author is more happy than Curtius in reproducing in all its freshness the very life of ancient times.

tion of their tutelar deity for the treasures of the state.

Among the various fragments of ancient edifices which strew the Athenian hill of the gods, you find in front of the eastern portico of the Parthenon, where excavations have been recently made, drums of columns in various stages of preparation, and the remains of a small circular temple, with the inscription on its entablature, "To Rome and Augustus." A rude hut near by contains a collection of ancient lamps, vases, pottery, and fragments of sculpture. Even the struggles of Turk and Greek have left their memorials in bones and skulls, with which a deep pit is filled. But your attention is most worthily attracted by the exquisite slabs from the frieze of the Parthenon which lie against the wall, on the pavement of the temple itself, or among the piles of fragments against the Propylæa. Beautifully unstained and white, and surviving in almost the full glory of their original perfection, there is something exceedingly touching in them as they lie carelessly in those piles of ruin. Nor will you disdain to pause for a moment and admire the loyalty of an owl, whose rude and quaint, but grave and impressive image, is perched among these relics, still faithful amidst the desolation of his mistress's fane.

Nature asserts her charms, on this the very throne of Art. How often did I turn from living frieze and swelling column, to gaze entranced upon broad plain, and calm, majestic mountain, and sparkling, blue, blue sea!

But, however reluctant, we must leave this consecrated rock, for Athens has much else to show. Glancing, as we descend, at the high pedestal which stands in front of the Pinacotheca, and formerly sustained a statue of Agrippa, we will mount that craggy height directly opposite the western end of the Acropolis, and distant from it but two hundred yards, — the hill of Mars, — haunted not only by the associations of the most venerable tribunal of Athens, but by those, more impressive still, of the sublimest scene which even this city ever witnessed, — one of the sublimest scenes in the history of our race, — the confronting of the simple truths of the Gospel of

Christ with the pomp and pride of Grecian philosophy and religion, when Stoic and Epicurean gathered around to hear the strange teachings of the Apostle to the Gentiles. Undazzled by the beauty of shrine and statue, "his spirit was stirred in him, when he saw the city wholly given to idolatry"; he knew how much corruption was mingled with these rites; he knew that this religion, however much it ministered to the taste, was unable to cleanse the heart and the affections, and satisfy the deepest wants of the soul; he knew, too, that though God had overlooked "the times of this ignorance," He had been pleased, "by that Man whom He had ordained," to reveal the full knowledge of Himself, and proclaim that catholic faith which was to be embraced by every nation, tongue, and people, — a faith loftier than the most spiritual dreams of Plato, wider than the broadest generalizations of Aristotle, — bringing with it a happiness and internal peace unimagined by the Epicurean, a heroism of soul and a superiority to the accidents of time unknown to the Stoic. He had "disputed in the synagogue with the Jews and with the devout persons, and in the Agora daily with them that met him"; and now the curious philosophers, longing to hear him unfold his new and strange belief in greater quiet and to more advantage than in the thronged square, led him to the Areopagus. He mounts the rudely excavated steps which lead up the rocky hill. Though short, and prematurely bent in person, there is on him the unmistakable stamp of greatness; his eyes are quick and piercing, but kindly and sympathetic; his nose bold and aquiline; his beard thick, and already sprinkled with white: * evidently a strong, earnest, impetuous, but sensitive and loving spirit. About fifty years of age, he is at the meridian of his intellectual strength. Peril and hardship have deepened the furrows on his brow; but his wan features are aglow with holy ardour, inspired by his single purpose to proclaim, among the baffled seekers after wisdom, "the power and the wisdom of God."

* On the personal appearance of the Apostle, see Edwards's Encyclopædia of Religious Knowledge, Art. "Paul."

He ascends to the levelled platform of rock on which the Court of the Areopagus held its sessions; near him, on the brow of the hill, is a temple of Ares; immediately below him, in a cleft in the rock, the dark sanctuary of the Eumenides; above him tower the temples and statues of the Acropolis; around, in whatsoever direction he turns his eye, it falls upon the shrine or statue of some one of those gods whom the hospitable mythology of the Athenians received in greater numbers, and whom they worshipped with more devotion, than any other city on the earth. He opens his mouth, but it is not to utter the words of fanatical denunciation. Nay, he commends the Athenians for their obedience to that instinctive impulse which leads man to bow down before the conception of divine power: widely apart as stand their systems and his, in this elementary principle they meet at one: and, having conciliated his hearers by the recognition, so far, of the legitimacy of their worship, he proceeds to point out its misdirection, and guide them to its true object. "Ye men of Athens," he says, in words of masterly rhetoric, no less than of sacred and momentous import, "I perceive that in all things ye are much inclined to reverence divine power. For as I passed by, and beheld the objects of your worship, I found an altar with this inscription: To the Unknown God. Whom therefore ye worship, though ye know him not, him declare I unto you." The Apostle was interrupted by cries of derision, before he had given utterance to all that burdened his heart; yet how comprehensive his speech! How significant, beneath the shadows of the Parthenon, and almost at the feet of the idol statues of Phidias, the declarations that God "dwelleth not in temples made with hands," and that "we ought not to think that the Godhead is like unto gold, or silver, or stone, graven by art and man's device"; how apt the quotation, from "certain of their own poets,"

"For we are also His offspring"!*

---

* This half-line, *τοῦ γὰρ καὶ γένος ἐσμέν*, is found both in the Hymn to Zeus of the Stoic Cleanthes, and in the Phænomena of Aratus, an astronomical poem. Two other quotations from the Greek poets were made by the learned Apostle; viz. 1 Corinth. xv. 33:

And although, "when they heard of the resurrection of the dead, some mocked," and to many of that throng of Greeks the doctrine of Christ crucified was "foolishness," the seed was not sown that day in vain; "certain men"—among them an honourable member of the council of the Areopagus—"clave unto him and believed"; nor was it without instruction for all future time that the picture has been given us in the sacred record, of the proclamation, in the proudest seat of human philosophy, of the revealed mysteries of Christian truth.

Turn we from the stand of the sacred messenger whom Longinus enumerates among the masters of Grecian eloquence, to that Bema from which the secular orators of Athens launched their thunderbolts. The Pnyx, or place in which the parliamentary assemblies of the people were held, lies on the gently

---

φθείρουσιν ἤθη χρήσθ᾽ ὁμιλίαι κακαί,

from the Thais, a comedy of Menander; and Tit. i. 12:

Κρῆτες ἀεὶ ψεῦσται, κακὰ θηρία, γαστέρες ἀργαί,

from Epimenides, the Cretan prophet and poet.

sloping side of a low, rocky hill of limestone, thinly clad with herbage, about a quarter of a mile west of the Areopagus.* A platform of rock, nearly semicircular, with an area of twelve thousand square yards, was the simple gathering-place of the Demos. No seats were provided, except a few wooden benches in the first row, but the citizens stood, as in Faneuil Hall, or sat upon the bare floor of rock. With no canopy but the vault of heaven, they chose the morning hour for their meetings, before the sun's rays should become oppressive. A vertical wall, made by excavating the solid rock of the hill, forms the southern boundary, and is the chord of the segment; the ground slopes gradually from this wall to the circumference of the area, in whose lowest point, near the centre of the arc, is built a terrace wall of huge polygonal blocks, fifteen feet high, within which the depression has been filled. Projecting from the middle of the southern wall is the

* Distinguished scholars have disputed the correctness of this site; but, after examining the arguments on both sides, it seems to me that the propriety of placing it here is established by a strong concurrence of probabilities.

Bema, — a stand or pulpit, of rectangular form, twenty feet high, and eleven feet broad at the top, widening at the base into seats, which rise three or four in number above each other, and its summit reached by a flight of steps. It were long to enumerate the objects of immortal renown which met the eye of the orator as he stood upon this block; nothing was wanting that could remind him of his country's greatness and her fame. Nor need I recount the visions which rise before the mind of the scholar as he stands on this haunted rock, — the mighty shades of orators and statesmen,

> "Those ancient, whose resistless eloquence
> Wielded at will that fierce democratie."

The rock wall at the side of the Bema is full of tiny niches for offerings, and various little marble representations of different parts of the body have been found in the neighbourhood, here hung, as are similar images before the shrine of a favourite saint in some Catholic churches, and dedicated to Zeus Hupsistos. We are not to wonder at this consecration of the ground devoted to political assemblages; it is in complete accordance with the "religiousness" of the Athenians, which "made of every public place and building a sanctuary."

Passing over the hill of the Nymphs, crowned by an excellent astronomical Observatory recently built by the liberality of a wealthy Greek residing in Austria, a short walk brings us to the best-preserved relic of the great days of Athens, the Temple of Theseus,* — at once the temple and the tomb of the mythic founder of the Athenian form of popular government. It is a memorial at the same time of the hero's friend, Heracles, and of the alliance between the cities which the two represent, Athens and Argos. The ten metopes of the eastern front were adorned with sculpture representing the labours of Heracles, while only eight (the four adjoining the eastern front on either flank) commemorated the

* This temple is of the Doric order, of Pentelic marble, with six columns at each end, and thirteen on each side. It is about thirty years older than the Parthenon. Its length is one hundred and four feet, breadth forty-five, and height to the summit of the pediment thirty-three and a half. The stylobate is mounted by two steps, instead of three, — a fact which, as has been suggested, may indicate its inferiority as an heroum to a temple.

exploits of Theseus. None of the other metopes were ornamented; but both the eastern and western pediments were filled with sculptures, known only by the traces left of their metallic fastenings. The remains of the metopes, and of the friezes of the pronaos and posticum, are of a bold and noble style of art. The color of the marble walls and pillars of the Theseum, as of the Parthenon and all the old ruins of Athens, has been changed, by long and gradual oxidation, to an "autumnal hue," — a mellow golden brown, so rich and satisfying that one would not exchange it for the whiteness of stone freshly quarried.

Very appropriately, this temple is now occupied as a Museum of relics of ancient Greek art. Statues and reliefs, — often dating from the best periods, and of great beauty and significance, — and a collection of inscriptions of more or less interest, are sheltered within its walls. They were picked up or excavated in the city and its neighbourhood, or, in some cases, in distant parts of the kingdom. I have vivid memories of the grace and beauty of some of these statues, but regret that my notes are not full enough to justify any attempt to describe them; — indeed, under the best circumstances, what adequate description of either a painting or a statue can be given in words? Particularly noteworthy are the reliefs upon the marble gravestones, the noble workmanship of the followers of Phidias. These represent some family group, — most frequently a husband and a wife, but often with the addition of other members of the domestic circle, — and are generally taken to represent "l'adieu suprême." With that delicate feeling, however, which in language led the Greeks to abstain from words of ill omen, and to soften the expression of everything disagreeable, the sculptor represented none of the painful features of the parting hour; not from the couch of sickness extends a wasted hand, but the departed wife or husband stands or sits in the full bloom and vigour of health, and clad in the garments of every-day life. A child may be gazing into that face which is soon to be hidden in the tomb; attendants may hold before it an unconscious infant; but there is nothing to denote death rather than life, except a silent sorrow, a sad foreboding, delicately impressed on every countenance, and immortalized in the marble, in the calm repose of perfect art. The right hands of the two principal figures, extended towards each other for clasping, or actually clasped, speak plainly of parting; but it is the happiness of life, to be darkened by that parting, and not the hideousness and ghastliness of death, which is represented: — so different in spirit are Greek art and Teutonic. Comparatively humble as they are, these sepulchral monuments can boast the characteristic merits of the statelier sculptures of the Parthenon frieze, — an unaffected naturalness and simplicity, an exquisite delicacy and refinement, a depth of meaning, told by the simplest touches, and a power of breathing the breath of life into marble, in which the sculptors of Athens, if ever equalled, can never be surpassed.

The monument of Aristion, an old Marathonian warrior, is one of the most noteworthy in this collection. On a high and narrow pillar of Pentelic marble is carved, in low relief, the figure of the worthy hoplite, armed with cuirass and greaves and helmet, and grasping a long lance in his left hand. Sturdy and stalwart, he makes the battle of Marathon a reality. With a certain stiffness, there is a remarkable truthfulness and vigour in the delineation of the various parts of the body; and while the artificially curled hair and beard, and the set smile on the lips, remind you of Assyrian sculptures, there is a life and freedom in the whole effect, which you recognize as a gleam of the untrammelled inspiration that, breaking all bonds of conventionality in the spontaneous play of genius, created the subsequent wonders of the Phidian age.

The decided traces of colour in this ancient work have a particular importance in the history of painted sculpture. They confirm the opinion, that "only ornaments as ornaments, and those portions of the body in which nature herself passes from the simple flesh-tone to more decided colouring,—as the eye, the hair, the lip,—were accessible to colour, never the flesh as flesh."

Plunging into the tangle of the modern town, you find in the yard behind an humble house a singular statue,—perhaps of Erichthonius,—represented as a man to the middle, thence a dragon with a fish's tail. The chest is vigorous and bold, the muscles strongly marked, but the joint between man and dragon abrupt and unskilful. In a cellar near by, I saw a similar statue (then recently discovered and but partially excavated), lying horizontally, and forming part of the foundations of the house. There are some interesting architectural remains of the Roman period in the midst of the town,—the portico of Athena Archēgetis, consisting of four Doric pillars sustaining a pediment, bearing an inscription recording that the building (of which these are the only remains) was erected by means of donations from C. Julius Cæsar and Augustus,—and the rich Corinthian columns of the Stoa of Hadrian.

In the outskirts of the modern city, on the southeast, stands the Gate of Hadrian, inscribed, on the side facing the Acropolis, "This is Athens, the ancient city of Theseus"; on the other, "This is the city of Hadrian, and not of Theseus." It formed an entrance to the enclosure of the great Temple of the Olympian Zeus, whose ruins, if without the peculiar interest which invests the monuments of Ictinian and Phidian art, are among the most beautiful and imposing in the world. They consist of an exquisite group of pure Corinthian columns, of Pentelic marble, rising to the height of above sixty feet, and by rare good fortune so unencumbered and remote from incongruous objects as to keep the charm of their grace and their stateliness unimpaired. Fifteen of these columns, the loftiest of their kind in marble in all Europe, still stand in their original places, while a sixteenth, blown down in a storm in the autumn of 1852, needs only the replacing of its stones to be as perfect as before. But where are the rest of the one hundred and twenty columns, — where the walls of the colossal temple?* It is almost

* This temple of Jove, which Livy speaks of as "the only one in the world undertaken upon a scale commensurate with the majesty of the god," was three hundred and fifty-four feet in length, and one hundred and seventy-one in breadth. A double range of columns at the sides, and a triple range on either front, made up the peristyle, which had ten columns on each

inconceivable how the depredations for building material, made in the Middle Ages, could have exhausted such a quarry.

The charm of this stately group of columns is all their own, for they boast no such fascinating associations as those which cluster around the ruins on the Acropolis. Begun by the tyrant Pisistratus, and finished seven hundred years afterwards by the Roman Emperor Hadrian, the Olympieum, though one of the grandest temples in the world, seems hardly a part of the glory of Athens, — breathes not her peculiar spirit, nor is redolent with

---

front, and twenty on each side. There were also three columns between antæ at each end of the cella. The exterior enclosure was about half a mile in circumference.

The columns were more than six feet and a half in diameter, and above sixty feet high. Each one (as I found by examination of the prostrate pillar) is fluted with twenty-four channels, the regular number, and composed of twenty-one cylindrical blocks, whose upper and lower surfaces, at which the different blocks come in contact, are polished to extreme smoothness, except at the centre, where a little circular space is left rough and uneven; near the exterior two cramps of iron are inserted, opposite each other, by which the drums were joined firmly together. These inner surfaces, not having been exposed to the air, are of the most exquisite whiteness.

the aroma of her soil. Yet Grecian hands have hewn those shafts and shaped those lovely capitals, and Nature, "adopting them into her race," has given them on this broad plain a home second only to the rocky pedestal of the Parthenon in its fitness to display and enhance the loveliness of its inhabitants.

You find here the same rich, mellow brown or iron-rust hue, the same weather-stains and battered edges, as in the other ruins. A modern excrescence will attract your eye, on the architrave above one of the columns, — the remains of a little cell of brick, once inhabited by a monk emulous of the fame of St. Simeon Stylites. The odour of his sanctity attracted old women around his dizzy perch, and they kept him supplied with food, which he drew up in a basket. A young guide who accompanied me in my first strolls about Athens, and prided himself on his linguistic accomplishments, told me, as he pointed out this cell, "There was a monk*ee* used to live up there." I did not correct his English in this instance.

Modern Athens uses the open space around the Olympieum as a pleasure-ground. Here on any pleasant afternoon or evening you will find Greek men and women, in their peculiar dress, seated at tables picturesquely grouped among the ruins, and partaking of cakes and wine or coffee, furnished from a shop close by. Men and youths, hand in hand, their red caps flashing and blue tassels waving in the air, dance along, singing Greek songs in nasal strains of Chinese-like music. Perhaps a mother leans against one of the columns, with her son's head in her lap, while she rids him of "certain personal companions." And some donkey, feeding or carrying a load in your neighbourhood, gives utterance ever and anon to the prolonged, unearthly vocal agonies for which that beast is remarkable.

A massive buttressed wall of large blocks of stone supports the platform on which the temple stands, and separates it from the lower ground which slopes down to the Ilissus. This classic stream is but a scanty brooklet, although the width of its bed and the depth of the channel attest its occasional importance when swollen by the rains. It is crossed, at the point where you would strike it on walking down from the Olympieum, by a tasteful modern bridge of white marble, with three arches. Above lies the little pool and fountain of Callirrhoe, whose waters trickle from beneath a bank of rocks, which are themselves picturesque in their varied outline. Ascending the stream, you walk upon its dry bed of sand and pebbles till you have come near the Stadium, — where I again found water flowing in the channel, — and you reach the piers of the ruined bridge which here in old time with a hugh arch spanned the stream. Then, stepping across the Ilissus, you enter the long hollow between precipitously rising hills, where was the Stadium Panathenaicum, the scene in the classic age of many a feat of strength and speed, sometimes imitated on the same spot in these degenerate days. The hills themselves, aided by excavation and by artificial constructions of masonry, make the walls of the edifice, in the form of an elongated horseshoe.* Their sides were lined with marble

* The length of the Stadium was six hundred and seventy-five feet, its width one hundred and thirty-seven feet at the lower end, but nearly twice as great at the rounded end, where the chariots turned.

seats, which have now totally disappeared, accommodating twenty-five thousand spectators, while multitudes more could stand above, and view the games. A winding passage-way through the hill, near the upper end of the Stadium, mercifully afforded the means of an unnoticed exit to the unfortunate competitors who were distanced in the race.

We have nearly completed our survey of the most important ruins of Athens; but there are still places, whose very names are spells of potency the world over, that we must visit. Let us first, returning along the Ilissus, and crossing past the southern side of that rocky height, the pedestal of the Parthenon, ascend the hill Musæum, which lies a short distance to the southwest of the Acropolis. Here we shall be detained a few moments by the ruins of the sepulchral monument of Philopappus,—a work of the age of Hadrian, adorned with statues and sculptured reliefs not without merit. But a deeper interest attaches to some hewn chambers in the rock at the base of this hill, called the "Prison of Socrates." They are three in number, and the inner chamber has a funnel-shaped dome, with a round aperture letting in the light from the top. However doubtful the tradition which has given these excavations their popular name, no traveller will regret to be reminded of a scene so impressive as the death of that inspired heathen, who, when he was confronted with his judges, and when he conversed with his friends before his execution, taught that we should recompense to no man evil for evil,* and that no evil can happen to a good man living or dead.†

And, having ennobled ourselves with the memory of Socrates, let us seek a fitting place to pay our homage to his greatest pupil. A walk of a little more than a mile, in a northerly direction, will lead us to the Academy. Our road, after leaving the town, passes through low vineyards and olive-groves, watered by little streamlets led from the Cephissus. A gentleman's garden and summer residence now occupy the site of the grove of Academus. A few little marble posts, a few fragments of statues and architectural ornaments imbedded

* Plato's Crito, 49.

† Apol. Soc., 41 D.

in the wall of a reservoir, are all that indicate the structures with which it was adorned; but beautiful trees here wave their branches, and sweet flowers bloom as of old. Look up, and beyond the wide meadow and the town, that stately Acropolis

> "Her pillared wreck of chastest shrines
> Upholds serene and still."

The gardener at my visit plucked me a handful of white and red roses, — a graceful offering to a stranger from remote Atlantis.

We may extend our walk a short distance northwards to two little hills, which rise to the height of about a hundred feet above the plain, and mark the site of the Attic deme Colonos, immortalized in song. On one of these hills a marble monument points out the grave of that profound and genial scholar, Karl Ottfried Müller.

The flower of all my memories of Athenian grace and beauty is the recollection of my last night in the violet-crowned city. I had seen my last sunset from the Acropolis, gilding that varied picture of sea and shore. Hymettus, at whose feet the vale of Athens nestles, had put on, for my delight, his evening robes of lilac and violet, Pentelicus his kingly purple, and Lycabettus his beaming gold. In the soft twilight I walked from hill to hill, and ruin to ruin, to bid farewell to their now familiar charms. And when the moon, then near her full, had rolled a flood of silver radiance over the scene, I bent again my reverent steps to the Parthenon, — explored every corner, every stone, — rambled over the hill, to different points of view, or sat on fallen columns, or in the marble chairs of the Areopagites, now brought up to the temple. And while for hours I drank in the beauty of harmonious forms revealed in white light and tender shadows, or indulged the dreams which the associations of the place inspired, a deeper feeling of gratitude filled my heart with thanksgiving, and hallowed my delight.

EXCURSIONS.

ÆGINA.

Beautiful Ægina, the old rival of Athens, lies in full view from her hills, at the distance of about twenty miles from the Peiræus. One fine morning in the last of June, I joined a party on an expedition to this island. It was a company calculated to appreciate the full interest of what would be seen; there was my old companion, the Professor, — my messmate, the indefatigable scholar, — and a young German artist, with the gift of song, employed by the Queen on paintings for the palace. François, the most learned, intelligent, and agreeable of Greek guides, again accompanied us as *factotum*. We drove before sunrise to the Peiræus, making our way outside the town, to the right, to a little cove where a sail-boat with two oarsmen had come to meet us, thus evading the port laws which allow no boat to leave the harbour before ten o'clock. By the way, the navigation laws of the Greek kingdom are very injudicious, and tend, by their foolish restrictions, to throw a great part of the carrying trade into the hands of the foreign steamers which ply between the Greek ports. A good breeze bore us rapidly along, and in two or three hours we landed on the northeast side of the island, where we saw excavations in the rocks just covered by the water, and other indications of the existence of a port there in ancient times. We walked to a garden a little way from the shore, looking greener than the greater part of the land in the neighbourhood, and there, among grapevines and under a broad fig-tree, took our lunch.

François talked with us about his nation, and expressed decidedly his disapprobation of the King, for his personal, as well as his political qualities; "for," said he, "he is deaf, he squints, he lisps, and he has no children!" But we were impatient to reach the temple, which we had seen to good advantage before gaining the shore; its graceful pillars, on the summit of a considerable elevation, being beautifully relieved against the sky. We climbed the hill, which is dotted with pretty bushes and small trees, and found the remains of the temple quite noteworthy, — twenty columns of the peribolos and two of the cella standing entire, and still surmounted by the architrave. Drums of the fallen columns lay scattered here and there, in the most picturesque confusion; and the green shrubs on the sloping sides of the hill, the view of vales and heights in the interior of the island, and the all-glorious prospect of the sea and the Attic coast from Sunium to Salamis, made up, with the beautiful ruins, a scene of unusual interest and variety. The stone of which the temple is built is of a light gray colour, and porous. Where exposed to the storms, it has been considerably worn and eaten. It was covered with stucco, — now almost entirely worn away, — and, in parts, beautifully painted; the walls of the cella were vermilion-red, the tympanum azure, the architrave adorned with yellow and green foliage, the triglyphs blue, the guttæ of the same colour, and the fillets above them red. The upper mouldings of the cornice, and the roof, were of marble. We were disappointed in the size of the temple. The pillars, seen in the clear air at a distance, from the sea, give the idea of a much larger building than is actually found.*

Leake still maintains the old, and certainly the most grateful belief, that this is that renowned temple of Zeus Panhellenius built on the spot where the prayers of Æacus, the most pious of mankind, appeased the wrath of heaven, and stayed the plague of famine and barrenness with which the gods had smitten all Greece. But the opinion advanced by Stackelberg in 1826, that it was dedicated to Athena, has met with general favour among scholars. I fancy that the artist who was with us, and who carried away a beautiful sketch of the lovely ruin, cared little about its name. With the hill it crowns, and the magnificent prospect of sea and shore which it commands, this temple has furnished the subject

* The temple was ninety-four feet in length, and forty-five in breadth. It was peripteral, having six columns on each front and thirteen on each side.

of some of the most beautiful of modern paintings. One by Turner, in the possession of an English nobleman, which I saw in an exhibition in London, struck me as one of the most satisfactory and admirable of that great master's productions.

The pedimental sculptures dug up in front of the temple in 1811, and skilfully restored by Thorwaldsen, are the best examples extant of pre-Phidian art. No traces of them are now to be found on the spot, but I saw and studied them in Munich, where they are preserved in the Glyptothek as its greatest treasure. They had been broken, many of them, into so small fragments that their restoration was a miracle of skill. The sculptures of the western pediment are the better preserved, but those of the eastern were wrought in a higher style of art. In the western group the subject is the fight of Greek heroes, chiefly of the race of the Æginetan Æacus, with the Trojans, for the dead body of Patroclus (or, as some will have it, of Achilles) ; in the eastern, is represented the fight of Hercules and Telamon the son of Æacus with the Trojans, for the body of a fallen Greek, probably Oicles. Athena presides over both combats, forming the central figure in each pediment; a fact favouring the hypothesis that the temple was built in her honour. In the older sculptures (of the western pediment) we find something of the stiffness and angularity of early art; the muscles, too, are exaggerated, the proportions of the figures remarkably short, the hair is elaborately curled, and every mouth wears a smile. But the joints and sinews are accurately defined, and a conscientious, careful aiming at truthfulness to nature is conspicuous throughout, even in the exaggerations. Again, in the life of the attitudes, and the spirit of the grouping, as well as in the truthful anatomical delineation of the different muscles and members, an immense superiority to Ninevite and Egyptian art appears, and the unequalled skill of the Greek begins to be manifest. In the sculptures of the eastern pediment, the defects of the old style have nearly vanished, except in the heads; and the anatomical truth of representation is astonishing. But five figures remain of this eastern group. Among them two are particularly admirable: a nude warrior advancing, with outstretched arms, — a figure which in perfection of anatomical treatment, and in lifelikeness, ease, and meaning, can hardly be surpassed, — and a wounded, prostrate combatant, — probably King Laomedon, who was slain by Hercules, — a sculpture not unworthy of comparison with the Dying Gladiator.

The figure of Athena in the western group (but small fragments of her statue on the eastern pediment are preserved) is a little more rigid and less expressive than the others, having the archaic character of the hieratic style, — the Greek sculptors of that period deeming it their duty to adhere as closely as possible to the old traditionary representations of their deities, which were hallowed by time and by sacred associations, but, being the creations of a less advanced age, were deficient both in anatomical truth and in expression of intellectual life.

In that part of the island which we saw, the soil was dry and scorched, and the vegetation scanty. There were, to be sure, one or two carob-trees, and many figs and olives. Ants were numerous, but we met none of the Myrmidons. A man or two in the fields, and a few boys watering donkeys at a well in a hollow, were the only human beings that encountered us on old sea-ruling Ægina, "the stranger-thronged Dorian island."

The wind had gone down when we got again upon the water, and we had to depend on our oars to return. The long passage was enlivened by pleasant talk, and songs both Greek and German. Our Greek song was an improvisation by the Professor, who imitated capitally the nasal unearthly intonations and Chinese rudeness of Modern Greek singing.

PENTELICUS.

At about half past eight on the morning of the 14th of May, we started — Clyde, Nixon, and myself — for a drive from Athens to Pentelicus. Our kind companion and guide boasted the classic name of Odysseús Kynēgós. The sun gave unwelcome earnest of his mid-day fury ; yet we rode comfortably through vineyards, olive-gardens, and wide fields, whose dry, thin soil, though barren and untilled, was fragrant with aromatic herbs, and gay with red poppies, rose-coloured mallows, white and pink convolvuli, daisies, and bright yellow flowers. Gradually rising from the plain, we arrived at length at a delightful grove of tall, handsome silver-poplars, with a clear babbling brook running through it, — thrice welcome both, in that parched and treeless land. How we revelled in the shade, and the coolness, and the greenness, — in the music of the water and its refreshing draughts!

> "Te flagrantis atrox hora Caniculae
> Nescit tangere, tu frigus amabile
> Praebes."

After a lunch in the grove, we walked to a ruinous monastery just above it, in whose court-yard grew a noble laurel of great size, and whose chapel is adorned with Byzantinesque pictures of sacred personages, quaint and stiff, — as are all the productions of the school of Mount Athos, — but not without feeling.

A monk conducting us to the proper path,

we began the long, hot, laborious ascent of the mountain. We passed the quarries in which the sculptures of Phidias slept unconscious before his hammer and chisel knocked off the encumbering marble and brought them into the light. Bits of marble of dazzling whiteness, scattered all along our path, reflected the sun with a blinding glare. We found mica-slate abundant, and some specimens of delicate rosy and white quartz, and crystals of calcareous spar. Pentelicus is a mass of compact limestone or marble, resting on a stratum of micaceous slate, "of unknown thickness," which seems to form the base of all the mountains of Attica. The juniper and the arbutus, prickly oaks, lentisks, and bays, clothe the sides of the mountain, which were also plentifully besprent with yellow immortelles. Stopping now and then where we could find a little shade under the bushes, we refreshed ourselves with juicy oranges, — a provident thought of Clyde's, which I recommend to all mountain climbers in hot countries. But at length poor Kynēgós's heart failed him, at the foot of a very precipitous crag which we had to scale, and he turned back to await us at the monastery.

"Hills peep o'er hills" on Pentelicus, as on other mountains; but after several lessons on the vanity of human expectations, we planted proud, conquering feet upon the topmost height, and forgot our toil in the enjoyment of the glorious prospect.* First in interest was the view of the plain of Marathon, the general topography of which can here be studied to great advantage; the knowledge I gained of it stood me in stead, when subsequently, with an incompetent guide, I visited the field itself. Lovely indeed is the natural scenery which human deeds have clothed with such interest. The sweep with which the bright beach of silver sands curves into the crescent of the Cynosura is exquisitely charming. Beyond, from the blue waters, rose Eubœa, with its hills of picturesque outline softened in the

---

* Pentelicus is, next to Parnes, the highest mountain in Attica. Its summit is 3,637 feet above the sea; that of Parnes 4,592, Hymettus 3,340, and Lycabettus 903.

summer haze. We traced the four passes to the field of Marathon, one on the north beyond the marshes, two at the west, and one at the south by the sea. Nor were we insensible to the beauty and thrilling interest of the whole panorama, — mountains and valleys, and islands and sea, — for the whole of Attica lay at our feet.

A cairn has been built on the summit by the contributions of successive travellers; to which we did not omit to add each our stone. Descending, we dined in that Elysian grove, where the simplest fare was nectar and ambrosia, and then dashed back through the thyme-scented plain to Athens, the never-satiating Acropolis before us all the way.

THE MODERN CAPITAL AND KINGDOM.

"Another Athens shall arise,
And to remoter time
Bequeath, like sunset to the skies,
The splendour of its prime."

SHELLEY.

MODERN Athens presents in its aspect the same incongruity, the same intermixture of barbarity and civilization, as the modern kingdom and people of Greece herself. Its nucleus is a confused, dirty, ill-built Turkish village, of narrow, crooked lanes, and low huts without windows; beyond this has grown up a modern European capital, with regular streets and neat and handsome houses, in comfort and elegance worthy of the nineteenth century. A solitary palm rises above the shabby post-office, and is a graceful feature in every view of the city. Near it, on a high tower, is the only public clock, the gift of Lord Elgin. The streets of Æolus and of Hermes, which intersect each other at right angles, are the principal thoroughfares; they are both straight, except that the latter curves gently in one part to avoid a picturesque little church, in quaint Byzantine style. There are several other Byzantine churches in the city, of considerable antiquity and no little architectural interest. Of the modern buildings, the Palace is the most pretentious; it fronts a fine square at the western end of Hermes Street, and is sufficiently ugly on the exterior, looking like a long, dreary barrack; the interior, however, is bright with painting and rich with marble. A better taste has been displayed in the University, which has a fine marble Ionic portico, successfully adorned with colours and gilding about the capitals and in the sunken compartments of the roof. The new Cathedral, of Byzantine architecture and built of marble, though unfinished at my visit, gave promise of a stately edifice.

Of productive industry there are few tokens. The people in general find plenty of leisure for idling at cafés or walking about. Their favourite promenade is along Æolus Street, in its northward continuation beyond the city to the little suburb of Patissia, a distance of a little over half a mile. It is a dusty road, with nothing attractive immediately about it, but it affords a delightful view of the long and picturesquely involved range of Parnes in front, while on the left you have the blue Ægean, soft, yet metallic in its lustre, and beyond in the distance the Peloponnesian hills, on the right bold Lycabettus, and behind you that grand, "vast altar," the Acropolis. On every pleasant evening the promenade is frequented, but on Sundays the whole population crowd it: tall, slender youths from the University — pale and thin, many of them, but some of superb beauty — swing along in an independent gait, their waists laced excruciatingly tight; priests, in long robes of black and black caps, and with long hair and beard, mingle in the throng; gentlemen and ladies on horseback, both Greek and foreign, and families in carriages, dash by; till all collect around a stand in an open area to the right of the road, whence a military band discourses music. On such occasions, the King and Queen, when they were in the city, seldom failed to join the circle, well mounted, to listen to the performance and exchange salutations with their subjects.

You will notice here, and wherever you meet the people, that the men almost invariably carry a rosary, whose beads they are continually telling and twirling in their fingers, — but not for any purposes of devotion; for this is only an ingenious expedient by which the Greeks avoid the question, sometimes troublesome in the polished society of Western nations, "What shall gentlemen do with their hands?" The lounger in the café, the tradesman behind his counter, the judge on the bench, and the senator in the Boulē, all preserve the equilibrium of their nerves and muscles by means of this regulator.

Landscape gardening has not been attempted except in the Queen's garden, in the rear of the palace; but here with decided success. In the evenings of June days of suffocating heat, I found these grounds a most delightful resort, and refreshed myself with the costly verdure of their turf and foliage, and the beauty of their flowers, so grateful in contrast with the parched and bare appearance of all other ground in the neighbourhood. Amongst other treasures, the Queen prided herself on her oleanders, of many colours, and often with double flowers. Fortunately, remains of a Roman villa were found here, and its mosaic pavements, surrounded with living walls of flowers, give additional interest to the garden, which can also boast — what is indeed one of its chief attractions — a near view of the columns of Olympian Zeus.

The aspect of Greek affairs is more encouraging on the side of intellectual than on that of material progress. In provision for the education of the people, Greece has been more liberal than some of the foremost nations of Europe. Her demotic or common schools in every village, her "Hellenic schools," (in which ancient Greek, Latin, and French are taught,) and her gymnasia in the larger towns, and, crowning all, her University, with its able corps of upwards of fifty Professors, its library of nearly a hundred and twenty thousand volumes, and its six hundred students, constitute a complete apparatus .for the instruction of her future citizens up from the first lessons of childhood to the highest fields of science.

The University of Otho (its designation indicates only that Greece had a German monarch, not that he manifested any extraordinary liberality in endowing her institutions of learning) attracts students from all the islands and shores of the Ægean. It is, indeed, the eye of the modern Greek race, and second only to the Greek Church as a rallying-point for the sentiment of nationality. Besides the regular students, the lectures are attended by many of the citizens of Athens, who manifest a very general thirst for knowledge. Judging from those I heard, by several of the Professors, the lectures at the University of Athens in interest, ability, and scholarship will not compare unfavourably with those at similar institutions in Western Europe and America.

Excellent provision is made for the instruction of young ladies, as at the schools of Madame Mano and of the American missionaries, Dr. and Mrs. Hill, to both of which, as to the

University also, pupils are sent from all the regions in which Greeks have made their home. No lover of his race can contemplate these efforts for the diffusion of education without cheerful hopes for the future of such a people.

To bind the race together, and maintain its own consciousness of its unity, — to perpetuate, amidst the shocks of conquest and the degradation of bondage, the Greek language, Greek ideas, and, in substance, Greek nationality, no instrumentality has been more potent than that of the Greek Church. There is something extremely imposing in the image which this venerable organization presents to the mind. The oldest division of the visible Church, reading the Scriptures, both of the Old and the New Testaments, in the same language in which they were read by the Apostles, and observing the remotest (unbroken) traditions of ritual and usage, — if the husk were the thing of value, and not the kernel, well might she claim allegiance and conformity from the whole Christian world.*

---

* President Felton, in one of the notes to his edition of

Yet undoubtedly in the very antiquity and orthodoxy on which she vaunts herself lies one of her greatest dangers: that of narrowness and formality, infacility of adapting herself to the changing features of changing times, and excessive reliance in the dead letter rather than in the ever-living Spirit. But the independence of that division of the Eastern Church which is comprised within the limits of Greece herself, the better provision therein made for the education of the clergy, and the contact of the East with the West in

---

Lord Carlisle's "Diary in Turkish and Greek Waters," quotes a writer in the *Spectateur de l'Orient* as follows: —

"If one of the holy fathers of the Council of Nicæa, — if St. John Chrysostom or St. Basil should return to life on earth, — in what part of the world, except here, would he find the Christian Church of their times? At the mass, at the ceremonies of baptism, of marriage, etc., they would acknowledge that not an iota has been changed; that they find in their places even the sacerdotal vestments, even the sacred psalmody, as if more than fifteen centuries had not rolled away since their time."

I grant that this antiquity is illusive. It runs back only to a period of ecclesiastical corruption, in which the simplicity of the primitive churches had been sadly departed from. But it runs back further than that of any other existing external organization.

the advancing civilization of the new kingdom, must gradually give its faith a broader, more catholic, and more intelligent spirit. The inevitable strife between "High Church" and "Broad Church," Old Greece and Young Greece, has already been inaugurated. The former party have very recently attempted to check the distribution of copies of the Holy Scriptures amongst the people; but there is no danger of their gaining more than a temporary success, if indeed they succeed at all. It is a boast of the Eastern Church, that it has allowed, if not encouraged, the free circulation of the Bible, and that its non-Greek communicants are permitted to translate its service into their own language. Among those of its features which are most open to criticism, a Protestant would notice the tedious length of its service, the infrequency of preaching, and the deficient education of the clergy. The latter defect bids fair to be materially obviated in Otho's recent dominions.*

---

* That the Eastern, as compared with Western Churches, exhibits the peculiarities of the Oriental mind, has often been remarked. An extract from the beginning of the shorter

The language, though mutilated in its grammatical forms, and corrupted by the accretion of foreign words, is still Greek, — the same language substantially as that of Homer, Demosthenes, and the Greek Fathers, with less alteration than might have been expected from the shocks of foreign conquest and mediæval barbarism. Any one tolerably familiar with classical Greek can take up an Athenian newspaper, or a book in the modern language,

---

Catechism, used in the schools of Greece, will illustrate the comparatively metaphysical tone of its teachings.

"*Concerning God and His Perfections.*

"*Q.* What is it necessary that he should know first, who wishes to know God?

"*A.* He must know himself.

"*Q.* Why?

"*A.* Because, when a man has examined himself, he perceives that it was impossible that he should have created himself.

"*Q.* And what dost thou infer from this?

"*A.* That he was created himself, and all other creatures, by one uncreated Being, the which is God.

"*Q.* Hast thou other proofs that there is a God?

"*A.* The first proof is this world, which we see made with so much wisdom.

"*Q.* What is the second?

and read nearly everything on the page. A half-hour's study of Professor Sophocles's Modern Greek Grammar, to inform him of the chief peculiarities of the new dialect, and ordinary ingenuity in guessing the meaning of novel words, are the only assistance he need desire. To enable him to read the popular songs, however, and understand the conversation of the common people, a dictionary will sometimes be requisite; and in the use of the

---

"*A.* The common confession of all nations that are found in the world; for all, in common, believe that there is a God.

"*Q.* What is the third?

"*A.* Our conscience, which rejoices for the good works that we do, and grieves for the bad.

"*Q.* And what is inferred from this?

"*A.* That there is one All-seeing and Almighty Judge, rewarding virtue and chastising wickedness.

"*Q.* What is the fourth and final proof that there is a God?

"*A.* The inborn desire which we have for a perfect happiness, which, however, it is impossible that we should obtain in this world.

"*Q.* And what is inferred from this?

"*A.* That our Creator, God, would not have implanted such a desire in our soul in vain, had he not intended to satisfy it in the other life with the supreme good, which is God himself."

13

spoken language, he will be obliged to habituate himself to the peculiar modern pronunciation.

In literary activity, if not in intellectual achievements, the Athens of to-day repeats the Athens of old. She publishes more newspapers, in proportion to her population, than any other city on the globe; * and her scholars are beginning to produce respectable and elaborate works in literature and science.

But there are many obstacles yet in the way of national regeneration.

Purblind diplomacy never blundered more palpably than in the negotiations which determined the boundaries of the new kingdom. False notions of the importance of doing as little injury as possible to the power of Turkey excluded much that was rightfully entitled to independence, and by nature a constituent part of the Greek state. Thessaly, the cradle of the race, the first Hellas, — and still

---

* Of the Greeks, as a people, even before the Revolution, Mr. Finlay remarks: "It is probable that a larger proportion could read and write than among any other Christian race in Europe." — *History of the Greek Revolution*, II. 20.

inhabited by a more unmixed Greek population than most parts of Otho's kingdom, — the birthplace of Rhegas, the patriot bard, and the home of many of the foremost champions of the Revolution, — with its rich soil (whose annual bounty Greece so much needs), its intelligence and thirst for knowledge, and its fitness for freedom, — this Thessaly and Epeirus were both thrust back under Mohammedan despotism. What a commentary on the sagacity and the fairness of the diplomatic map-makers of Western Europe! From the necessity of the case, this first misstep has entailed others; and in the Crimean war France and England were compelled to crush by their arms the efforts of a gallant people to vindicate their freedom and nationality, and secure a higher civilization. Honest Lord Carlisle, who was on board one of the English vessels sent on an expedition "to the Macedonian and Thracian coast, to show the flag, encourage the Turks, and prevent any improper communications from Greece," betrays his consciousness that they were playing a strange part for Englishmen. "Our mission here, indeed," he says, "is to give countenance to the invaded Turks, and the reverse to the insurgent Greeks. Such, probably, is loyally our duty; still the thought recurs, where are we now doing this? — opposite the Pass of Thermopylæ." *

But Greece has found worse obstacles than unnatural boundaries. She has still to wait for wise and liberal rulers.

It was a day of proud hope for Hellas when, escorted by the fleets of three great nations, her youthful monarch landed on her shores.† A graceful youth of seventeen, manly and prepossessing, with a reputation for kindness of heart and quick intelligence, ‡ — no wonder

---

* "Diary in Turkish and Greek Waters," p. 263, American edition.

† February 6, 1833.

‡ N. P. Willis, who was presented to King Otho at Nauplia, a few months after his landing, thus describes his appearance: "He is rather tall, and his figure is extremely light and elegant. A very flat nose and high cheek-bones are the most marked features of his face; his hair is straight, and of a light brown, and with no claim to beauty; the expression of his countenance is manly, open, and prepossessing." The same writer, in speaking of the young king's visit to the American frigate United States, says, "As he stepped on the deck,

that every eye followed him with admiration, and every heart with blessings, as he rode to his palace through joyous throngs of his new subjects, hailing his advent as their deliverance from an anarchy no more tolerable than the tyranny of the Turks which preceded it. Nor can we doubt that Otho then sincerely desired, as he continued to the end to desire, the happiness and prosperity of his people. But, educated in a petty German court, with feudal notions as far remote as possible from applicability to the affairs of Greece, and, notwithstanding his honesty of purpose, by nature

---

and was received by Commodore Patterson, I thought I had never seen a more elegant and well-proportioned man." Mr. Finlay says of the new sovereign, "Though not handsome, he was well-grown, and of an engaging appearance."

Commander Wise ("Harry Gringo"), who was in Greece at the same time as myself, paints him as he was then. "Otho is tall and slim, with a small head and very large neck; dark hair, flat nose turned up at the apex; no front teeth, and somewhat hard of hearing; in fact,

'So very deaf,
That he might have worn a percussion-cap
And been knocked on the head without hearing it snap.'

But still, with his German-grayish eyes, the face is, on the whole, pleasing."

narrow-minded and obstinate, he has failed to satisfy the expectations which the establishment of Grecian independence had reasonably excited in his nation and the world. Singularly blind to the truth that all national greatness must rest on a groundwork of material well-being, he has done next to nothing in the way of opening roads, reclaiming lands, planting forests, or fostering the interests of agriculture and commerce. Trained in the narrowest maxims of bureaucracy, he has perpetuated the evil work, begun by Capodistrias, of crippling the municipal institutions of the country. Yielding with ill grace in 1843 to the demands of the people for the constitutional government which had been promised them, he has to a great extent neutralized its advantages by tampering with the elections, and filling both houses of the legislature with his creatures. Errours so grave cannot be counterbalanced by the good qualities with which they coexisted, or by the benefits which could not fail to result from the substitution of any kind of regular government for anarchy. It is not to be wondered at that the

Greeks were dissatisfied with their "barbarian" sovereign, and that his reign was checkered with many a revolt.

Sagacious kingcraft has always allied itself with the religious prejudices of the people. Yet to the Greeks, so proudly Orthodox, the Great Powers sent a Catholic King, who took to himself a Protestant Queen. It was in the bond, it is true, that their children should be brought up in the tenets of the national Church; but the hopes which the people entertained for an heir to the crown born on Greek soil and educated in the Greek faith have been disappointed. We may set it down to the credit of Otho, that his was not the easy virtue of Henry IV. or of Bernadotte, and that he remained true to the faith of his ancestors; but, as enlightened England wisely excludes from her throne all who shock her prejudices by professing either his religion or that of his recent subjects, so it might have been expected that Greece would be restive under a king of a different creed from her own, and it is not strange that the want of religious sympathy between him and his people was one of the causes which led to the deposition of the Bavarian dynasty.

Perhaps the capital errour of the Greek government has been the retention of the Turkish land-tax, which exacts yearly one tenth of the produce of the soil, and is so burdensome in its operation that it has effectually checked the development of the agricultural resources of the country, preventing the immigration of labourers and the building up of a sturdy and independent yeomanry.

But the Greeks should not forget that, great as is the influence of the government upon a nation, much more must always depend upon the people themselves. If the energies which have been wasted in rebellion had been devoted to the peaceful discussion of measures of reform, and the dissemination of sound principles, or to the promotion of a better training, both in the family and in the school, something would have been done to secure that elevation in the character of the whole people which is the sure bulwark of freedom, and which, by its moral influence, must sooner or later compel despotism to give way.

And so also of those hopes — not, as I believe, unfounded — which contemplate fondly the vision of a Hellas with enlarged boundaries, and with a power which shall not be insignificant in the councils of Europe. To the few who, from personal interest, may read these words on the banks of the Ilissus, and to all the statesmen and patriots of Greece, if my voice could reach them, I would say with all earnestness, Labour manfully for the education of your people, not only in the learning of the schools, but in those habits of industry and thrift which are best calculated to develop your material wealth, — that integrity and honour which shall gain them the confidence of other nations, — that sturdy morality, without which national stability is impossible, — that generous aspiration for well-regulated liberty which shall make them render a cheerful obedience to constituted authority, whilst they strive persistently, but by peaceful measures, to effect the removal of all restrictions which obstruct their progress. Piedmont had gained the respect and confidence of the world by her quiet career of well-ordered liberty and wise national development, before she sprang forth to rescue Italy from tyranny, and add the fairest to the countries of the free. Greece, too, must educate herself up to the height of the full desert of freedom and of greatness, before she can hope to welcome "the rich dawn" of her "ampler day." She must find her Cavour before her Garibaldi.

Let her show herself worthy, and Thessaly, Epeirus, and Macedonia, Crete and the Ionian Isles, shall be hers in fact, — and by moral gravitation, rather than through bloody convulsion, — as they will be hers by divine right, — that right which consists in the evident and providential fitness of things, attested by common interests, hopes, and aspirations, and by the invincible consciousness of a common nationality.

THE DISCOVERIES AT ATHENS AND MYCENÆ IN 1862.

In the spring of 1862, some eminent German scholars had the happiness to make discoveries in Athens which will mark an epoch in the history of archæology. The additions thus made to our knowledge are so important, that I am unwilling to leave the foregoing chapters without appending some notice of them.

And first, the Dionysiac Theatre has been in great part laid open to view, by the removal of the soil and rubbish which covered it to the depth of twenty feet. The excavations were conducted by Mr. Strack, royal architect of Prussia. They disclosed the seats occupied by the general body of spectators, and moreover a number of marble thrones or chairs of honour, next to the orchestra, and constituting the three front rows. The chairs still bear the inscriptions designating the officials for whom they were designed, so that, as Curtius says, "if the dignitaries of the city were to come back to-day, there would be no quarrels about precedency of seats to fear." * It is a striking fact, that, of the chairs of honour thus far excavated, almost all — or forty-one out of forty-five — were designed for priests or men of sacerdotal rank. "This may be accidental, since certainly many more of these chairs have been destroyed than preserved, and conspicuous seats for the magistrates could not have been wanting; yet, on the other hand, the extraordinary insignificance of many of the deities whose priests are named in the inscriptions (such as the Muses, Eucleia, Eunomia, and certain obscure heroes) makes it probable that an extensive claim on the part of sacerdotal personages to seats in the theatre was early made, and was subsequently turned to account by means of half-illusory priestly titles." † At any rate, especial dignity and

* "Festrede" before the University at Göttingen, June 4, 1862, p. 10.

† E. Gerhard, in the "Anzeiger zur Archäologischer Zeitung," May and June, 1862, p. 328; from an article on the discoveries in the Dionysiac Theatre, to which I am indebted for my best information on the whole subject.

prominence was given to the priests at the theatrical representations, — a consequence perhaps of the religious character which actually belonged to the dithyrambic and choral odes from which Greek tragedy took its origin, and which continued to be attributed to the drama itself.

The midmost and most highly decorated of the chairs was appropriated to the priest of Dionysos. It is adorned with reliefs of satyrs and winged genii. On one of the bench-rows, as it appears from an inscription, seats were reserved for the guild of stone-masons. Besides the chairs and rows of seats, two pedestals were discovered, a colossal female statue without head, some remains of the *scena*, and the ascent from the orchestra to the middle of the *proscenium* (the stage, in modern phrase), on the upper step of which is carved the following inscription of the Roman period : —

" Fór thee, wild-revelling god, this beautiful stage was erected
By Phædrus, Zoïlus' son, bountiful Attica's archon." *

The investigation of the ruins on the Acro-

---

* Σοὶ τόδε καλὸν ἔτευξε, φιλόργιε, βῆμα θέητρον (sic)
Φαῖδρος Ζωΐλου βιοδώτορος Ἀτθίδος ἀρχός.

polis, with their inexhaustible problems, was intrusted to the skilful hands of Professor Bötticher. He has established the fact, that in the Parthenon there were two doors between the cella, or the Hecatompedon, and the Opisthodomus, having actually detected the sockets in the floor wherein the pivots were inserted upon which the doors turned, the scratches made by the rubbing of the doors against the pavement as they were opened and shut, and even by the bolt which fastened the doors against the sill, the hole into which this bolt was inserted, and the marks of feet which passed over the threshold. Each of the doors was five feet wide in the clear. They were folding-doors, and were fastened on the side of the Opisthodomus.

Bötticher has also found sufficient confirmation of his hypothesis of the existence of a platform or raised seat for the magistrates and judges, before the statue, whence the prizes were bestowed in the Panathenaic festival, "whilst a select festal assembly filled the space of the cella beneath, and from the upper galleries, to which the steps on both sides of the Parthenos mounted, resounded hymns of victory and joy." * The statue itself is proved to have been placed further back than previous investigators have supposed.

The door of entrance to the Opisthodomus from without, Bötticher finds to have been a double one, the halves of the outer door opening against the sides of the aperture in the temple-wall, which was six and a half feet thick, and the inner door, of brazen lattice-work, opening directly into the Opisthodomus. Above the door was a very large latticed window.

In the temple of Athena Polias, Bötticher has discovered six windows in the crypt, and arrived at a theory of the structure of this whole building, differing from any hitherto entertained. For fuller information in regard to the result of his researches,† I await impatiently the appearance of a book which he promises upon the Acropolis, in which we may expect a fuller and clearer exposition than

* Curtius, Gr. Gesch., II. 274, 275.

† My information in regard to Prof. Bötticher's discoveries is derived chiefly from extracts from his letters from Athens in the *Arch. Zeitung* for May and June, 1862, pp. 321 – 324.

has ever yet appeared, not only of the outward form, but of the internal organism and structure, — the whole anatomy of the different parts and their respective functions, — in those wondrous architectural creations on the rocky citadel of Athens, which, in the immortal beauty and perfection of their design and meaning, in spite of all the mutilations to which they may be subjected in their outward form and embodiment, will remain a *κτῆμα ἐς ἀεί*, a possession for all time.

Not less interesting than the brilliant discoveries of Strack and Bötticher were those made by Professor Curtius, who undertook a thorough investigation of the most important points in the topography of Athens.* It does not fall within the scope of this little volume to follow this distinguished scholar as he traces the whole history and development of the city on the ground itself, points out the seats of the earliest inhabitants, determines the boundaries of the Agora and the course of the city walls, and re-creates the Athens of the past

---

* See extracts from letters from Curtius, etc., in the number of the *Arch. Zeitung* already cited, pp. 324 – 327.

with a skill equal to that of the geologist and the palæontologist in restoring bygone epochs in the history of our globe. But I am bound to lay before my readers the decisive results of his excavations at the so-called Pnyx, in which he has disclosed the whole of the old polygonal wall, hitherto in great part hidden, and proved that the original surface between this wall and the " bema " was of rock, carefully levelled and sinking as it receded from the bema, and therefore not intended to be covered with earth. That the present surface is not the old one is further proved by the discovery of the foundations of middle-age buildings upon the original ground, and of three steps hewn in the rock beneath the brick masonry of these foundations, as well as by the finding of shards of pottery, terra-cottas, bits of inscriptions, and two fragments of votive offerings, — the latter being naked members of the human body dedicated to Zeus Hupsistos. Moreover, trenches were found, smoothly cut in the rock, and dividing it in a manner inconsistent with the hypothesis that this was the place wherein the political assemblages of the people were held. And so, as Curtius says, instead of hopelessly pursuing the quarrel on the modern surface, the original ground has been for the first time interrogated, and a final answer in the negative returned to those who have asserted the claims of this locality as the veritable Pnyx. Yielding perhaps too easily to the conservative arguments of English and American scholars, I have myself indulged the *gratissimus error* that I had planted my feet upon the rocky tribune whence Pericles and Demosthenes first uttered those words which will echo through all generations; but the science which wins so much for us from the scanty relics of the past, may well be forgiven if it sometimes dispels our pleasing illusions.

On the slopes of the Musæum, also, Curtius undertook excavations, whence important information may be derived; and at the Munychia topographical investigations were set on foot which promise the richest results. Scholars will read with eagerness the full account of his researches which Curtius has promised in his "Attic Studies," the first number of which was to appear at Christmas, 1862, in the Proceedings of the Göttingen Academy of Sciences.

The old-time monuments of Mycenæ were not neglected amidst the archæological attractions of Athens. Mr. Strack, accompanied by Professor Vischer of Basle and Mr. Schirrmacher, an architect, devoted several days to their examination. Of the relief over the Gate of the Lions Strack declares that all the drawings that have been published are false; that the pillar (as he proved by actual measurement) is not smaller at the bottom than at the top, but of uniform diameter throughout; that the lions stand on two separate pedestals, and not on one with a hole in the middle; and that the architrave above the capital does not exhibit balls in its middle portion, "but cylindrical figures like tree-trunks." The concurrence of all previous beholders in representing the pillar as growing smaller towards the bottom, proves that there is an optical illusion in the case, as indeed might be expected in a column of uniform diameter, our eyes being accustomed to columns larger at the bottom than at the top. The heads of the lions, as Strack states, were inserted by means of stone pegs ; inasmuch as they were turned outwards, and the stone tablet on which the bodies were carved was not thick enough for the heads to be wrought in the same piece of stone.

On the northwest side of the walls of the citadel, the explorers laid open a gallery with a pointed-arched roof, like those of Tiryns, " so that now all the forms of Pelasgic construction are found in Mycenæ." They also explored the remains of the smaller vaulted subterranean building, near the "Treasury of Atreus" and resembling it in construction, where they uncovered fourteen circular courses of stone, and found a brazen plate of the lining of the inner surface still well preserved.

Under the auspices of the Royal Museum at Berlin, plaster casts have been taken of a number of hitherto uncopied sculptures, among which are the lions from the gate of Mycenæ, and the monument of Aristion.

The researches so happily begun will doubtless be continued. The Archæological Society of Athens has taken in hand the completion of the excavation of the Dionysiac Theatre, and German scholars will not abandon the seat of their triumphs till every problem of its archæology has been either answered or proved unanswerable. Meantime, in all civilized nations the results of these investigations will be watched for with interest; for wherever the achievements of the noblest powers of man are held in honour, everything will be welcomed that throws new light on the history and the monuments of Hellas.

NOTES.

P. 17. How painful would it have been, at this entertainment on board the Cumberland, to have foreseen the civil strife in which that noble vessel was to gain its sad immortality!

P. 130. Curtius discovers in the frieze of the Parthenon a representation not so much of the actual procession in the Panathenaic festival, as of the preparations for the same. Had it been the task proposed to give a true copy of the procession itself, he says, "all freedom would have been taken away from the inventive artist; a solemn monotony would have been unavoidable, and every representation of this kind would have remained as a feeble counterfeit far behind the living reality. Much more significant was it to represent the preparations for the great festal procession; since therein the earnestness was manifested with which the Athenians undertook their national festivals. Thus, in a natural manner and without constraint, the groups of riders and the four-horse teams, the sacrificial trains and the musicians, the aliens performing service and the magistrates directing and marshalling the procession, could be represented." *Gr. Gesch.*, II. 267.

P. 134. The brilliant golden shields, with which the architrave was adorned below the metopes on the eastern and western fronts of the Parthenon, added to the varied effects of colour.

P. 140. Bötticher's recent investigations may give us greater certainty in regard to the much-disputed plan of the Erechtheum, and the purposes to which its different parts were appropriated. That a part of the temple was devoted to the worship of Poseidon, under the name of Poseidon-Erechtheus, seems to be established.

INDEX.

THE END.

Cambridge: Printed by Welch, Bigelow, & Co.

www.ingramcontent.com/pod-product-compliance
Lightning Source LLC
LaVergne TN
LVHW050527100826
845148LV00002B/472

* 9 7 8 1 4 2 5 5 1 9 4 7 6 *